DONALD J. PUTIN

ON AMERICAN EXCEPTIONALISM:
IT'S NOT YOU, IT'S JUST AMERICA BEING AMERICA

DONALD J. PUTIN

ISBN 978-1-7341267-1-6

Cover Concept: Ivanka J. Putin
Cover Design: Jena Brignola
Proofreading by Elaine York, Allusion Graphics/Book Publishing
www.allusiongraphics.com

To request permission to use passages from this work, please write to the author at Donald_j_putin@aol.com

DONALD J. PUTIN

ON AMERICAN EXCEPTIONALISM:
IT'S NOT YOU, IT'S JUST AMERICA BEING AMERICA

TABLE OF CONTENTS

WELCOME TO
AMERICAN EXCEPTIONALISM

T HIS BOOK IS NOT about Donald Trump. It is not about George W. Bush, or Ronald Reagan, or Bill or Hillary Clinton, or any "American leader" in particular. It *is* about American Exceptionalism. This is a loaded term: it means whatever the reader associates it with. Hence, the Fox News viewer might associate the term with God, Himself, decreeing that the white people of America have been specifically blessed to exercise their wasteful, greedy, racist, and greedy dominion over all of His creation and trash whatever they feel like and crap on whomever they feel like, because America. People more grounded in reality might understand the term as a pejorative reference to the arrogant refusal of the United States to align itself with such universally recognized, international cooperative efforts as the treaties pertaining to landmines, the rights of the child, and climate change (recently withdrawn from), or for its flouting of obligations, such as paying United Nations dues, or upholding the Geneva Conventions (not torturing prisoners, for example), or of course, for its undertaking of "preventive war." As used here, I simply mean the term American Exceptionalism literally. We will review how the United States is exceptional, as in an outlier from the rest of the world. In most cases, the United States is an outlier from its "peers;" its peers are usually considered to be the more "developed" countries of the so-called "First World" also understood as "industrialized democracies". In a surprising number of cases, the US is an outlier from virtually every other country on Earth. When I suggest that the United States is exceptional, I generally mean exceptionally *bad*. That is, the lives of the American people are more vulnerable, less happy, less satisfying, and simply *not as good* as people's lives in other countries. I suggest that this is the result of American Exceptionalism itself: that the unique origins and history of the United States of America, first as a European colony, and then as an independent nation, and then as a global empire, have resulted in this exceptional situation. This has serious implications. For the people unfortunate enough to be presently trapped within the United States, it means that they "enjoy" the world's highest incidence of anxiety disorders, the highest incidence of imprisonment, and being in a country that sports among the world's highest incidences of obesity, drug overdoses and gun violence, and some rather dismal, overall health and longevity outcomes. And this is despite the American people being, by far, the most profligate spenders on "health care" in the world. It means "enjoying" having the least paid vacation in the world (*i.e., none*) and being one of a tiny number of *all* countries *without* mandatory maternity leave and *with* draconian "employment at will" (*i.e.,* significantly fewer meaningful rights for employees than other arrangements of "employment with rights"). To be sure, there are many other areas where the US is most "exceptional." And we will discuss many of them. So, you ask, dear reader, what can I do about this? I humbly suggest to you that almost no one has been able to improve the fundamentals of the American system in four-hundred years, and *I ask you* what makes you arrogant enough to think that you can? Fortunately, there is an answer. At least as I write this in 2019, the United States will still give out passports to almost anyone capable of sitting still for a photograph, finding a birth certificate, filling out a form, and paying a fee. This is a good thing. Because it means that you can do the one thing that makes sense when dealing with an untenable situation. *You can leave.* I know: you may not be able to get work or immigrant authorization to move to the country of your choice. Most Americans insist that this be another "First World" country that speaks English, of which there are five that I can think of, in order of distance, Canada, Ireland, the United Kingdom, New Zealand, and Australia. You may be trapped by loved ones who do not wish to leave themselves. Or your loved ones may simply not be up for travel, let alone emigration. I find myself in this situation. To you, and to myself, I say, dip your toes in the water. Get out of the US as often as you can, even if it is only to Canada or Mexico, and walk around, breathe the air, and talk to people. If you can learn the languages of the places you visit, all the better; most people are delighted that you took the trouble to learn, even a little. Look at other people's faces, and observe that they usually appear more relaxed than most Americans. They probably have not deferred health issues for years out of fear of personal financial destruction. They probably move around relatively freely, without fear of being sued or arbitrarily arrested or shaken down. They probably get mandatory vacation time from their jobs, which, in turn, probably pay them a livable wage for their community. And they probably *have* a community.

Ponder all of this in the context of what you read. Think about your own personal inadequacies, and ask yourself how much they even have anything to do with you, or if it is just America being America. You may well choose to remain in the United States, even as it continues its slide to oblivion and desperately tries to take the rest of the planet with it. But then you will know that even thinking about reform or even the barest improvement of the American system is the most foolish of fool's errands. American Exceptionalism simply precludes such improvement. It would violate every core American principle. And you are about to find out why.

WTF?
(WHAT'S TO FOLLOW?)

T HE "ORGANIZATION" OF THIS entirely unambitious work begins with the Pledge of Allegiance in a typical American classroom, and then offers a brief history lesson of the origins of the United States, commencing with the white man's arrival in the 17th century. We discuss why this origin story is so important to understanding American Exceptionalism (hint: slavery). We move on to issues of childbirth and abortion policy. Then we return to school, move on to sports, entertainment, work, death and taxes, and, in the longest chapter, the history of the American empire. Yes, it is an empire. We talk about issues of sex as pertaining to women, "health care," guns, criminal "justice," and mass incarceration. We proceed to discuss suburban "life," poverty of spirit, faith-based initiatives (*i.e.,* what passes for American religion), social immobility (yes, that's a thing), food, sex, debt, the legal system, and finally, we close out with the scariest area of American Exceptionalism, the treatment of the natural environment. Some readers may believe that an accurate diagnosis is appropriate before treating the patient. I conclude that the patient is terminal, but do not let me stop you. I have tried to support my diagnosis with the data. Some of the data and some of my conclusions may be controversial. So be it. I am trying to help here by pointing out some "issues" in a system that is beyond help.

Assuming that what you read here rings true, you cannot say you were not warned. If it does not ring true to you, you probably

4

were not going to read it anyway. At least we can have a good laugh about it.

1. And So it Begins

T HE OFFICIAL PUBLIC INDOCTRINATION of American children in their "public" schools, the one universally available public service in the United States that does not involve people carrying firearms (or does it?) commences at the beginning of each school day with a recitation of the aptly named "Pledge of Allegiance." The pledge is actually codified into American law, found in Title 4 United States Code, or U.S.C., Section 4.

"I pledge allegiance to the Flag of the United States of America." Let us get the young Americans used to worshiping stand-ins and not addressing actual reality. Indeed, best avoid reality, even if that reality, a country or a political system or a geographic landmass or even a tribal grouping, is only itself symbolic of something else.

"And to the Republic for which it stands." We acknowledge that the American political system is not a democracy as most people you might ask on the American streets would tell you, erroneously thinking that Athenian self-governance is the American model. NYET! The American system is based on the centralized imperial Roman system, specifically its republican variant. The United States is, at best, a republic with democratic attributes. [1]

"One Nation under God." To hell with the atheists! To hell with the non-believers in American greatness and exceptionalism,

---

1   The US has fewer democratic attributes than you would think. A leading study from Princeton University has concluded that the modern United States is, in fact, an oligarchy, and only the will of the rich and powerful makes its way into public policy. *See* Gilens, Martin and Page, Benjamin, "Testing Theories of American Politics: Elites, Interest Groups and Average Citizens" (September 18, 2014) https://doi.org/10.1017/S1537592714001595

a group to which you, Dear Reader, will doubtless count yourself when you complete this, what I immodestly suggest will be a seminal exegesis on the subject of American Exceptionalism. Your knowledge of the subject will be based in reality, rather than upon propaganda. Uncritical acceptance of propaganda is something that Americans do better than anyone; a key part of the effectiveness of this propaganda results from telling Americans of their own personal inadequacy. From a young age, Americans are well versed in acceptance of the products of the dream factory of Hollywood, the lie factory of Madison Avenue, the dirty tricks factory of the CIA, and the blunt force factory of the Pentagon.

"Indivisible." Americans evidently feel the need to spare schoolchildren from the results of recent elections, or the unpleasantness of what passes for national discourse. This has been especially true since the United States outsourced its national discourse to an Australian maniac who then hired a bunch of well-coiffed, blonde Neanderthals to happy-talk fear and hate to angry and ignorant people.

"With liberty and justice for all." This expression is somewhat hilarious for a nation which was largely built by slaves and that maintains a prison gulag archipelago that incarcerates almost 1% of its population at any given moment, well over two million people in its prisons, jails, and detention centers, [2] more than any other nation or empire now or quite possibly ever.

Thus begins the lesson, Comrades. We start with an antecedent "key point," the one major source of distinction of the American system from its European peers. As a historical matter, American white people did not go through feudalism. Whether or not Americans went through feudalism is a subject of some academic discussion in its own right, [3] but I am focusing on *white people*, specifically,

---

2   See Segura, Liliana, "With 2.3 Million People Incarcerated in the US, Prisons Are Big Business: Meet the corporations who are profiting off our prison system," *The Nation* (October 1, 2013).

3   See, e.g. Hartz, Louis, "The liberal tradition in America: An interpretation of American political thought since the Revolution," Harcourt Brace (1955).

the descendants of English people who still form the "critical mass" of the American population. Non-white people, be they Native Americans or black people, Asian people or Latino people, generally *have* gone through some form of feudalism in the United States. This is particularly true if their forbearers were in the United States long enough. In many cases, many people of color may well be going through an unpleasant form of feudalism in the US *right now*.

This key difference—the lack of a feudal tradition for most of the American white people, who are still the majority of the American population—forms the backbone of American Exceptionalism.

The main consequence of American white people never going through feudalism is that the American system never established an embedded sense of *reciprocal obligation*. Thus, the powerful and rich feel that they owe nothing to the powerless and less well off. Nothing. And indeed, not only is there no established legal or structural framework for such reciprocal obligation, there is not even an "honor system" for this in the American context.

Mutual obligation, however, is the essence of the structure of proper feudalism. [4] Obligation in the American system, however, is *one-way*: this is entirely consistent with its most fundamental relationship, that of master and slave. A feudal lord, by contrast, knew that he was involved in an ongoing, complex relationship between his sub-lords ("vassals") and with his knights and peasants, all the way down to his serfs. All feudal parties would have understood that their relationships carried both rights and obligations. The lowliest serf knew that the lord could not just kick him and his family off the manor.

Early industrialists, principally in Great Britain, strived to undo the various civil and religious obligations endemic in British economic life through various structures that attached people to their land, even if only the right to live on and farm that land pursuant to centuries of tradition and obligation. Ultimately, the

---

4   See, e.g., Ross, David, ed., "Feudalism and Medieval Life," *Britain Express* (retrieved June 6, 2019) https://www.britainexpress.com/History/Feudalism_and_Medieval_life.htm

industrialists, especially in Britain, were successful in managing to undo much of the feudal tradition. This, in turn, resulted directly in extraordinary human misery complete with the poverty, disease, and penury made most famous in the Dickensian and high Victorian context. Still, the British industrialists could not completely eradicate "social obligation" from the British Isles. Hence, the mother country eventually established a modern social democracy, complete with social welfare including the popular National Health Service, free higher education (until recently), robust trade unions (until recently), strong worker protections, and so forth. At the same time, the United States remains exceptional in providing *little or none of this.*

As a thought exercise, we could go back to the roots of the modern American state, which are barely 400 years old. At the dawn of white man's America in the 17th century, the upwardly mobile scum of English society decided to break out of their otherwise decaying feudal relationships and travel, often involuntarily as a result of criminal conviction, to the seemingly virgin territory of the New World. Once there, they could acquire land that was not subject to the intricacies of feudal obligation. In many cases, they could become absurdly rich in a matter of years instead of many generations. Of course, the Americas were not exactly virgin territory so much as well-managed territory, the original permaculture if you like. [5] The caretaker native populations mostly and very conveniently succumbed to smallpox and other microbial infections, thus greatly reducing the trouble of having to slaughter any survivors in order to take their land. Where indigenous survivors proved intractable, the Europeans simply moved around them or waited them out, and *then* slaughtered them.

Native peoples proved rather difficult to negotiate with to perform European-style wage or contract labor needed to work backbreaking European-style cash generating agricultural ventures.

---

5   See, e.g., Grover, Sami, "How Native Americans Managed Wild Land Long Before Settlers," *Treehugger.Com* (April 26, 2011) https://www.treehugger.com/green-food/how-native-americans-managed-wild-land-long-before-settlers.html

Hence, it was most fortunate that there was a ready supply of landless Europeans, as noted, quite a few of whom were convicted criminals who gleefully accepted transportation in lieu of hanging. Of course, many of these Europeans came with issues. And fortuitously, someone discovered, particularly in the mosquito-ridden southern parts of North America, that African peoples were pretty good at working in those conditions without dropping dead from malaria and other diseases quite as quickly as many of the Europeans.

Of course, serving as a hard labor force thousands of miles from home was not exactly an arrangement that most reasonable people would seek out. Which is why, for the most part, they were abducted, sold into slavery and packed together as human sardines and sent on a transoceanic hell-ride that killed untold thousands or millions of them before they even made it to the American side. Originally, Africans were dispatched to work in similar indenture "contracts" as the Europeans as the colonies did not have laws permitting outright slavery for some decades after the arrival of Africans. [6]

But then the idea of a social pecking order with white indentured servants outranking black indentured servants took root. This quickly led to the development of American-style chattel slavery. This practice of "divide and conquer" *on racial lines* has been the model for American labor relations since the 1600s. Indeed, some form of divide and conquer has been the basis of virtually *all* American power relations ever since, whether between man and woman, enterprise and employee, police officer and member of the public, or between the state and subject; feel free to use the term "citizen" if you prefer to lie to yourself.

Once human chattel slavery was established in North America, the associated human trafficking operation became an incredibly profitable business in its own right, as did agriculture (of course). Significant to our discussion of American Exceptionalism, chattel slavery served as an excellent organizational model of the non-

---

6　　See, e.g., "Indentured Servants in the U.S.," PBS's *History Detectives* (retrieved June 6, 2019) http://www.pbs.org/opb/historydetectives/feature/indentured-servants-in-the-us/

reciprocal, neo-feudal arrangement that Americans still enjoy to this very day.

The "organization chart" should look familiar, as it has changed surprisingly little since the 1600s.

The native peoples generally had no place on the hierarchy, other than as the old tenants with the unfortunate habit of not moving far enough away.

The African slaves filled the role that otherwise would have been filled in Europe by serfs, only the Africans had far fewer rights (eventually none) and were the recipients of affirmative disdain and stigma based on the invention of white supremacy, another American social innovation duly perfected by the economic needs of the American elites.

Next up were the white European poor folk. This might be the most important group to discuss because they were then, and, at least in terms of their descendants, remain to this day, by far the largest group in terms of sheer numbers within American society. They often originated in the peasant class (some might have been serfs): mostly farm people who might (or might not) have owned or controlled their own land. Nonetheless, at least on the European side of the Atlantic, they would have lived amidst a complex set of mutual obligations between state, nobles, and church, all of which were largely absent in the "religiously tolerant" New World that offered all of that "free land." To be sure, there were vast economic opportunities resulting from the elimination of social obligation. These opportunities, coupled with the use of chattel slaves for further leverage, were enormous, and entirely unparalleled in "the Old World." For many new European arrivals, the myth of rugged individualism did not appear to be a myth. Whether they came intentionally or just to avoid being the main attraction at a public execution, they were giving up a complex and frequently oppressive set of obligations as well as an established place in the world in exchange for the simple rules of the New World: profit, or suffer, mightily.

For schoolchildren, in presenting "colonial life," much attention is focused upon the next group, the "middle classes" of various skilled tradespeople that did not specifically work the land, at least full time. These people either brought their trades from the Old World, or were fortunate enough to develop them in the Western hemisphere. We focus on the middle classes, of course, to perpetuate the myth that the United States is "a middle-class country." There were certainly profit opportunities for the middle classes in the Old World, although complicated guild arrangements and other social order factors (including taxation) could get in the way. Of course, this group usually had enough excess money and time and organizational skills to cause serious trouble to the top rungs of the social order if they were not happy. This is why many policies then and to this day exist for no purpose other than to keep the middle classes happy, even if these policies are often insanely expensive and inefficient.

At the top of the social hierarchy sat the land barons. Some of them rose from the peasant class in Europe and through hard work, luck, and ruthlessness, advancing from poverty in Europe to wealth in the New World, thus creating one of the most enduring myths of the United States ("land of opportunity"). To be sure, many, if not most, members of the land-baron class were reasonably wealthy Europeans who crossed the Atlantic to become substantially wealthier, whether intending to return to the mother country with more money, or to stay. Quite a few of these land barons actually brought noble titles with them; some of them bought their titles with the money they made in the New World. The more skilled members of the middle classes were well aware that the entire social hierarchy game was rigged for the benefit of the land-baron class, naturally, at the expense of everyone else. The peasants apparently were not so aware, or at least, did not act as if they were aware, one reason that, to this very day, class-consciousness has not developed in the US, a cornerstone of American Exceptionalism. This curious result probably arose because poor Europeans received the twin entertainments of looking down on the dark-skinned chattel slaves, and fantasizing about the myth of opportunity. As a result, the peasant class thought that the disposition provided by the New World hierarchy was the greatest thing ever, notwithstanding that back in Europe, their feudal lords had very real obligations to them such as seeing that food was available and that they didn't starve to death, obligations which were conveniently absent in the American context.

I offer you this brief historical discussion because without it, most of what we will discuss about American Exceptionalism will seem disjointed and nonsensical. NYET, Comrades! It is neither disjointed nor nonsensical. It is, in fact, the most brilliantly designed social system ever constructed.

Sadly, because active self-delusion is such an important component of it, it may quite possibly lead to the destruction of human life on planet Earth. This is because the vast bulk of Americans believe that a toxic, value-free existence fueled by the industrial and military might built up by their ancestors has provided them with the greatest country in the history of the universe. Part of this belief, despite all evidence to the contrary, is a belief that the US is not an empire, because empires do bad things and the Americans only do good and nice things.

So, away we go.

2. "I AM BORN" (OR AM I?)

THE FAMOUS FIRST LINE of *David Copperfield,* by Charles Dickens, is appropriate to our discussion for a number of reasons besides my personal admiration for Mr. Dickens as a writer. Dickens observed working conditions in Victorian England to which American employers have always aspired. He observed endless workweeks, dark and unsafe factories, child labor and low wages barely at subsistence levels. Ah, capitalism. Dickens also visited the United States in the mid-19th century, and observed its singular obsession with money; that has not changed significantly in nearly two centuries.

We also start with "I am born" because we have to start somewhere, and what better way to start our cradle-to-grave discussion of American Exceptionalism? Well, *I* have certainly already been born. I have a birth certificate to prove it. I strongly suspect that you have one, too. I intend to discuss *some* American baby being born *somewhere* to *someone*.

As of the first two decades of the 21st century, approximately two in five American babies are not born with benefit of clergy, *i.e.,* to a married couple. [7] This rate of birth outside of marriage—observe that "old school" right-wingers prefer the pejorative term "illegitimate"— is probably not terribly different in Scandinavian countries or other countries that, unlike the United States, provide a vast array of social

---

7   *See,* Clegg, Roger, "Latest Statistics on Illegitimate Births," *National Review* (October 4, 2012), https://www.nationalreview.com/corner/latest-statistics-illegitimate-births-roger-clegg/

services. In those countries, an unmarried woman knows that she can expect to receive social services from her own government. Thus, she knows that she and her child will not fall into immediate penury just because the father, who might even have adequate income and/ or wealth to support them, might not be ready, willing, or able to marry and raise a child with her. Such social services are generally unavailable, or at least available only with painful strings attached in the United States, especially after President Bill Clinton signed a law "ending welfare as we know it." [8]

Nonetheless, for a variety of reasons that probably exceed the scope of this already vast and ponderous work, I will limit my discussion of issues "I am born" in order to keep to the most salient points of American Exceptionalism.

We start with the difficult question of infant mortality. The United States, given the absurd amount of money that it spends on its health care system, is a disappointing (the correct term is "dismal") 29th out of 29 in infant mortality [9] among comparable OECD countries [10] . On the overall chart of *all* countries, the United States is ranked somewhere in the high 30s worldwide, at least according to Wikipedia, [11] still not very good.

The United States is vast. People in more affluent parts of it, such as New York or the San Francisco Bay area, are likely to have far better outcomes with respect to infant mortality and pretty much all other categories of health care outcomes compared to the less-affluent states, such as large parts of the American South. Further, there is the statistical matter of how to count "extreme premature

8   Vobejda, Barbara, "Clinton Signs Welfare Bill Amid Division," *Washington Post* (August 23, 1996) http://www.washingtonpost.com/wp-srv/politics/special/welfare/stories/wf082396.htm
9   Ingraham, Christopher, "Our Infant Mortality Rate is a National Embarrassment," *Washington Post* (September 29, 2014) https://www.washingtonpost.com/news/wonk/wp/2014/09/29/our-infant-mortality-rate-is-a-national-embarrassment/?utm_term=.888d08018f55
10   "The Organization for Economic Cooperation and Development (OECD) is a unique forum where the governments of 34 democracies with market economies work with each other, as well as with more than 70 non-member economies to promote economic growth, prosperity, and sustainable development." *What is the OECD, U.S. Mission to the OECD* (retrieved June 6, 2019) https://usoecd.usmission.gov/our-relationship/about-the-oecd/what-is-the-oecd/. "OECD" will be used periodically to describe major industrialized countries.
11   List of Countries by Infant and Under Five Mortality Rates, *Wikipedia* (retrieved June 6, 2019) https://en.wikipedia.org/wiki/List_of_countries_by_infant_and_under-five_mortality_rates

births." These are births many weeks or months before expected term, which carry an extremely high mortality rate. The United States counts these as "live births." A number of countries count such births as "stillborn," and hence, not part of their overall infant mortality statistics. [12] This, however, only explains part of the overall measure and position of the US. What, you might ask, *does* cause the mighty US and its health care spending juggernaut to have such exceptional, as in exceptionally bad, overall infant mortality? One possibility is maternal stress. The United States is proudly one of four countries, the other three being Papua New Guinea and the two landlocked South African enclaves of Swaziland and Lesotho, that do not provide for *any* form of mandatory paid maternity leave for mothers. [13] You, of course, recognize that the United States believes in rugged individualism! Hence, if women chose to have children, they can deal with the consequences on their own. These consequences include insanely high medical costs, loss of paid time from work in a country where four out of five adults live "paycheck to paycheck," and some rather unpleasant health consequences to mothers themselves, as the US also sports the worst maternal mortality rate in the developed world. [14]

For some perspective, if one is a member of the American ruling classes, such as corporate moguls, financiers, or land barons, or even from the middle classes, such as tradespeople and assorted credentialed professionals, there is a good chance that one's health outcomes will be well above typical American results. Perhaps they will even be on par with Europe, Japan, and other "First-World" countries that the United States pretends are its peers. For the rest, the mere middle class, the working class, and the actual poor, one's

12   Kamal, Rabah and Gonzales, Selena, "U.S.'s high infant mortality may be explained by differences in data, as well as health," *Kaiser Family Foundation Briefs, Health & Wellbeing,* (October 24, 2014) https://www.healthsystemtracker.org/brief/u-s-s-high-infant-mortality-may-be-explained-by-differences-in-data-as-well-as-health/#item-start
13   Phillips, Matt, "Countries without paid maternity leave: Swaziland, Lesotho, Papua New Guinea and the United States of America," *Quartz* (January 15, 2014) https://qz.com/167163/countries-without-paid-maternity-leave-swaziland-lesotho-papua-new-guinea-and-the-united-states-of-america/
14   Martin, Nina and Montaigne, Renee, "U.S. Has the Worst Rate of Maternal Deaths in the Developed World," *ProPublica/NPR Investigation* (May 12, 2018) https://www.npr.org/2017/05/12/528098789/u-s-has-the-worst-rate-of-maternal-deaths-in-the-developed-world

outcomes are less likely to be as favorable. Regardless of social class, the efficacy of medical care does not begin to address the monetary costs, which could well bankrupt a new mother or her entire family even before the child comes home from the hospital!

But, you ask, what if the lady decides to say "nyet" to an unwanted pregnancy? As I write this in the year 2019, the United States had had legally available abortion as a "legal right" since 1973. That year, the US Supreme Court issued a famous decision called *Roe v. Wade*, 410 U.S. 113 (1973). [15] Nonetheless, in the first few months of 2019, a number of states passed draconian anti-abortion laws [16] anticipating that a now favorable Supreme Court featuring Justice Brett Kavanaugh, himself accused of attempted rape of a young woman, would find such laws constitutional, or, at least, find an excuse to overturn *Roe* and re-criminalize abortion in much of the US. In practical terms, the government-sponsored medical care usually made available to poor people may not cover abortion procedures in many places in the United States. Indeed, while forcing a woman to carry an unwanted child to term seems draconian in any society, the often quite violent busybodies who concern themselves with whether *other* people can undergo a single medical procedure could not give the slightest care to the American big picture. They do not *care* that their beloved "exceptional" country fails to provide for paid maternity leave, for paid or even remotely affordable child care, or even for adequate assurance of food and shelter to young children or new mothers. Rugged individualism as practiced in the US is good and hard. Indeed, the same busybodies who protest this single medical procedure, conveniently obtained only by women, but who never protest any "men's issues" such as a psychotic gun culture (because America) frequently turn violent. Said protesters have shown a willingness to maim and kill to show just how "pro-life" they really are.

---

15   The numbers after a legal case name represent its citation as would be found in legal papers, specifically the volume number, official reporter—in this case "United States Reports" as signified by "U.S." and the page number, followed by the year of the decision.
16   Hutzler, Alexandra, "These are all the states that have passed anti-abortion laws in 2019," *Newsweek* (May 31, 2019) https://www.newsweek.com/state-abortion-laws-2019-list-1440609

The irony is that abortion opponents have essentially won, even before the day that *Roe v. Wade* is overturned by a controversial Supreme Court majority which would require the votes of accused attempted rapist Brett Kavanaugh and alleged sexual harasser Clarence Thomas. Abortion is presently unobtainable in something like 87% of the counties in the United States, simply because there is no facility in those locations in which abortion may be performed. [17]

If one has taken the trouble to get pregnant, and then to carry the child to term, she will eventually give birth to a child either blessed or cursed with, his or her parents' social and economic status, with little chance of escape. This is because the United States has become one of the world's most unequal nations in terms of distribution of wealth. [18] And in terms of social mobility, at least with respect to the extent that these things can be measured, Americans do not appear to have much of it anymore. [19] That poor women or even middle-class women might believe that they are not good candidates to raise a child, and thus might chose to abort their pregnancy is, however, the absolute biggest insult to *American capitalism* possible. Women who exercise reproductive freedom in this way would be voting with their uterus to hold back potential cannon fodder for the American military empire or for its industrial machine, or perhaps potential slave labor in the prison industrial complex. Indeed, because of legalized abortion, tens of millions of unwanted children *have simply not been born*. It is hardly a coincidence that abortion is such a staple of the so-called Republican Party, which is usually also thought of as the more "pro-business" and if you like, pro-"freedom" of the two right-wing parties in the American political duopoly, and, of course, the more right-wing one. While the American media pitches the culture wars as separate from "lunch bucket" economic policies, this is, of course, nonsense, delusion being an indispensable element of American Exceptionalism.

---

17   Florida, Richard, "The Geography of Abortion," *CityLab* (June 12, 2012) https://www.citylab.com/equity/2012/06/geography-abortion/1711/
18   Sherman, Erik, "America is the Richest, and the Most Unequal Country," *Fortune* (Sept. 30, 2015) http://fortune.com/2015/09/30/america-wealth-inequality/
19   Friedman, Howard Steven, "The American Myth of Social Mobility," *HuffPost*, (Sept. 15, 2012) https://tinyurl.com/y25ud26b

Now back to our story. The young lad or lass is born into their (usually maternal) parents' circumstances. To a shocking degree, in the allegedly richest and most powerful country on Earth, this means immediate penury. It often includes food insecurity; an estimated one in eight Americans suffer from food insecurity, defined by the United States Department of Agriculture as a lack of consistent access to enough food for an active, healthy life, including an estimated 12 million children as of 2017. [20] This takes place despite complicated and expensive government programs at all levels of American government intended to address it. Other issues facing an unfortunately large number of children and their families (especially working families) include housing insecurity and health care insecurity. For good measure, filial relationships may be abruptly interrupted based on the real or imagined behavior of their parents that could result in one or both parents being abruptly carted off to serve in the prison industrial complex. Around one in three black men receives this "opportunity." [21] Much of this arises from the "war on drugs" that is very good at both being a "war" in terms of violence brought to bear on communities, particularly communities of color, and at raging seemingly forever without any possible end in sight. Of course even without as dramatic a development as having one or both parents shunted to the penal system, the parents may have their employment and hence, their health care and housing interrupted for an infinite number of reasons. This is because the US is notoriously dreadful by world standards in protecting workers, or in providing them with meaningful benefits.

Even households of the middle and upper-middle classes often require both parents to work outside of the house just to afford housing, especially in some of the nation's most desirable metropolitan areas. And child care must be arranged, often at large, relative expense

---

20   "Understand Food Insecurity: What is Food Insecurity," *Hunger and Health: Feeding America* (retrieved June 7, 2019) https://hungerandhealth.feedingamerica.org/understand-food-insecurity/
21   Knafo, Saki, "1 in 3 Black Men Will Go to Prison In Their Lifetime, Report Warns," *HuffPost* (Oct. 4, 2013) https://www.huffpost.com/entry/racial-disparities-criminal-justice_n_4045144

to income earned. As long as there is still *some* income beyond child care, the two-earner household is required to maintain the arrangement, particularly on the East and West Coasts. And so the young lad or lass of the middle or upper-middle class will often find themselves raised not by mom, or even by daddy or papa or granny or pops, but by a paid stranger. In many cases, there may be an institution, often "a daycare center," involved. There, as suggested by blogger and author Dmitry Orlov, American youth will develop all the skills necessary to become a model prisoner of war. [22] Assuming that said young lad or lass has successfully completed potty training, they are ready to begin the first of their many official encounters with the American state, the "public school." Unless of course their parents are affluent or just plain lucky enough to be able to send them to a non-state arrangement for their education, or are "old school" or if you prefer, reactionary enough to demand to school their children "at home."

It is time for school.

---

22   Dmitry Orlov, "The Five Stages of Collapse: Survivors' Toolkit," New Society Publishers (2013)

3. School is In

THE OLDEST AMERICAN PUBLIC school, Boston Latin, was founded in 1635 and is still operating. Boston Latin is slightly older than nearby Harvard University founded in 1636. Somewhere in the 18th or 19th century, an idea took shape that the American citizenry needed to be adequately educated to maintain an informed electorate. Compulsory public education was born. It finally got going nationwide by the early part of the 20th century. [23]

While compulsory education was becoming compulsory, this did not generally interfere with traditional child labor practices associated with life on the family farm. Nor did it interfere with life on the sharecropper farm for those who did not have the good fortune to be white in the American southern states. Nor did it interfere with the neo-Dickensian conditions associated with factory labor in the late 19th and early 20th century. At that time, American industrial might was asserting itself to the world and attracting millions of Southern and Eastern Europeans who would rank below the white people already here, and attracting many Asians, who generally would rank below all but the black people.

To this day, American school scheduling is modeled on the agricultural laborers' calendar; summer is off because that is when

23   "11 Facts About the History of Education in America," *The American Board* (July 1, 2015) https://www.americanboard.org/blog/11-facts-about-the-history-of-education-in-america/

farm work tends to be at its most intensive, [24] although there are regional variations to account for planting, harvesting, and so forth. This is somewhat anachronistic, as the twin functions of the American school system as it now exists in the present century are to serve as a regularly scheduled child-care arrangement thus permitting industrial and/or service workers to perform their labors, and to get children used to the regimented industrial (or service) environment in which they will ultimately serve their betters.

Regardless of the school calendar's impact on the economy, John Dewey and other philosophers of his era convinced enough of the American elite to mandate public education for all. As it stands in the 21st century, all children must stay in school until at least their 16th birthday (assuming they are not diverted to the prison part of the school-to-prison pipeline). They have the right to stay in school until they graduate the 12th grade. One might think that a dozen or so years of organized learning would lead to a generally educated population. Instead, the United States ranks something like 125th in the world in "literacy," at least on one measure. [25] This gives one pause. Similarly, more specific rankings of American educational attainment, such as rankings of 30th in math and 19th in science, respectively, in the OECD and significantly lower overall among all countries, seem troubling. [26] This does not bode well, of course, for Americans' overall advancement in the industrial and post-industrial hellscapes now known as the American and global economies. Regardless of specific educational results, there seems to be consensus, at least on the political stage, that American schools are "failing." Because schools are failing, they need more "good teachers," and perhaps "the right incentives," notably "merit pay" and similar euphemisms for *money must be thrown at the problem.* Two

---

24   Pedersen, James, "The History of School and Summer Vacation," *Journal of Inquiry & Action in Education, 5(1)* (2012) https://digitalcommons.buffalostate.edu/cgi/viewcontent.cgi?referer=&httpsredir=1&article=1050&context=jiae
25   "List of Countries By Literacy Rate," *World Atlas* (retrieved June 7, 2019) https://www.worldatlas.com/articles/the-highest-literacy-rates-in-the-world.html
26   DeSilver. Drew, "U.S. students' academic achievement still lags that of their peers in many other countries," *Pew Research Center: Fact Tank* (Feb. 15, 2017) https://www.pewresearch.org/fact-tank/2017/02/15/u-s-students-internationally-math-science/

brilliant innovations are "charter schools" and "school vouchers." Charter schools prove that capitalism can achieve anything that the more traditional (*i.e., socialist*) model of public schools can achieve, only far more expensively. School vouchers, like charter schools, prove that for many Americans, the best way to deal with public schools is not to deal with them at all. Instead, the decision is made to divert money away from public schools (a "common good") and give the money to private and parochial schools. This works especially well for parents who believe that they are lucky enough to benefit from a charter-school lottery or from available vouchers. These innovations, of course, tend to skew the basic dichotomy between "public education" for the masses, and "private education" for the elites, by giving the hoi polloi the illusion that they are getting a superior private educational product at public expense. Obviously, there are degrees of segmentation within each category, as some schools in the private category are inner-city parochial schools that, while perhaps superior to nearby public schools that greet students with metal detectors and heavily armed "school resource officers," are nonetheless not quite the leafy campuses of public schools located in tony suburbs. Even the well-regarded suburban publics are still somewhat removed from the bucolic New England campuses of elite boarding schools, let alone their peers in Britain or Switzerland.

The irony is that regardless of which school is chosen, or not chosen, in the case of those who select "home schooling", the mission of the American school is remarkably similar. That mission, of course, is to train young people to prepare for a life reflecting the social standing of their parents.

Hence, for example, the elite are trained for prosperity and leadership. In many parts of the world, this would be commensurate with how *psychopaths* are created, but then, in the tooth and nail world of American capitalism, psychopathology is often a survival advantage. [27]

---

27   Clifford, Catherine, "Why psychopaths are so good at getting ahead," *CNBC.Com: Make It* (Nov. 18, 2016) https://www.cnbc.com/2016/11/18/why-psychopaths-are-so-good-at-getting-ahead.html

The next rung down on the American ladder of social hierarchy consists of technocrats frequently trained in "STEM" (science, technology, engineering, and mathematics). The "softer" of the technocrats, frequently, but not always, the girls, are duly trained in the "softer" realm of technocracy, such as the social sciences or the arts. These fields of study will, hopefully, assist them in their eventual posts in middle management, the law, accounting, or some other service essential to capitalism. Achieving such positions does not require that these well-trained technocrats share in the real fruits of capitalism. To be sure, they will likely get a nice-enough suburban tract house, two cars (assuming both mom and dad go to work as technocrats), a two-week annual holiday somewhere, and enough savings to feel like they have a stake in the system even though they really don't. Nonetheless, in the end, far too many people attend college in the United States to take advantage of the relatively few positions entailed by the available technocratic strata. We have reached the point where coffee and fast-food chains have created management tracks that pretend to require higher education. Indeed, the very colleges that spit out their graduates at tremendous cost, often imposing a lifetime of student debt, have themselves become a vast employer of last resort of the very people they graduate. This has created a huge administrative overburden that in turn requires ever-higher tuitions and attendant debt to maintain. Lather, rinse, repeat. The next rung on the social-hierarchy ladder is by far the largest, and consists of those students who fail to "graduate" from high school "on time" or perhaps at all, or do graduate, but only with marginal literacy and "skills." We often find such students in less-affluent parts of the United States. Here, too, the American education system has largely done its job of providing the requisite skills to its finished product, the American high school graduate. Such a graduate will comfortably fit into a lifetime of underemployment, video games, and gaming American social welfare. By the way, much of the American social welfare is not what you think it is. In fact, welfare recipients are often white people, and in programs not normally thought of as "welfare." For example, there are more people enrolled on Social Security disability, around 14 million, [28] than there are people who work in the American manufacturing sector, around 12 million. [29] Quite fortunately, members of this largest cohort of the American system are generally not expecting too much from the same system that failed their parents. Depending on the region, such students could receive an education in pro-Confederate "history" in their social studies class, or in "science" class, they could learn about "intelligent design," where a highly interventionist deity comes in and takes all the boring and technical parts out of biology, chemistry, physics, and earth science, and replaces them with wondrous miracles.

What American students in all but the elite or elite technocratic cohorts will *not* get is any kind of objective or particularly useful knowledge about pretty much anything. Which is why Americans' knowledge of the rest of the world—or even their own country— is a well- established joke. [30] We will certainly not discuss the typical Americans' poor proficiency with languages other than their own, [31] given that they seem to have enough problems with their mother tongue. Thus, American teachers fight a battle that they are preordained to lose before they start. Teachers attempt to impart knowledge and skills to their students so that they might actually *improve* their lot in life, when, of course, the system is designed to ensure that they only *maintain* their lot in life, which, for most American students is not to go anywhere, and so should not be so hard.

Nonetheless, dedicated American teachers still try to inspire young people to learn. Sadly, they often find that that a combination

28   Joffe-Walt, Chana, "Unfit for Work: The startling rise of disability in America," *NPR: Planet Money,* (retrieved June 7, 2019) https://apps.npr.org/unfit-for-work/
29   "Employment by major industry sector," *Bureau of Labor Statistics* (Oct. 24, 2017) https://www.bls.gov/emp/tables/employment-by-major-industry-sector.htm
30   Trevedi, Bijal P., "Survey Reveals Geographic Illiteracy," *National Geographic* (Nov. 20, 2002) https://news.nationalgeographic.com/news/2002/11/geography-survey-illiteracy/
31   "Europe drastically outpaces U.S. in foreign language learning," *Pew Research Center* (Aug. 6, 2018) https://www.pewresearch.org/fact-tank/2018/08/06/most-european-students-are-learning-a-foreign-language-in-school-while-americans-lag/ft_18-08-06_languages_europedrasticallyoutpaces/

of school administrators, politicians, union leaders, parents, senior but jaded teachers, and of course, poorly prepared students, will ultimately frustrate their efforts. This is most unfortunate. American teachers are part of a well-motivated, well-educated, largely female work force that, were it assigned a mission other than to hold millions of young people in their preordained social lot, might actually result in social mobility and dynamism. This was exactly what transpired during the mid-20th century when the needs of capitalism were consistent with the mission of gearing a population up for growth rather than for stagnation and decline. Nonetheless, teachers' current mission is very frustrating. Politicians love to pile on the canard that mythical "bad teachers" are somehow responsible for a problem that is not only not a problem at all, but represents the actual purpose of the system.

As a result, a huge percentage of new teachers burn out and leave the profession in short order; some estimates show that about half leave within five years. [32]

Still, even in the ossified confines of the American education system, there are still the occasional students who appear to soar above their circumstances, whether because they manage brilliantly of their own accord, or because they have encountered teachers who do not understand their mission. Such students might also thrive because of extreme and unexpected abilities, or just because of dumb luck. Who knows? For these overachieving students, we can at least try to discourage them at the next level. At that next level, the elite American colleges and universities will invariably reject them if they do not have a family member who is an alumnus, if they do not have sufficient athletic prowess, or if, for example, too many people from their region have already managed to get admitted.

If such students somehow evade the major college gatekeepers, the American system will nonetheless keep up its discouragement of all efforts at social mobility until it succeeds, and succeed it will.

We now turn to sports and entertainment.

---

32   Neason, Alexandria, "Half of teachers leave the job after five years. Here's what to do about it." *The Hechinger Report* (July 18, 2014) https://hechingerreport.org/half-teachers-leave-job-five-years-heres/

4. The Sporting Life

AMERICAN PARENTS ARE FAMOUS for enrolling their children in well-organized programs of sport. Among the most common of these sports is "little league baseball," where young boys try to throw a smallish white ball at other young boys as fast as possible without injuring their own arm, or perhaps killing the boy toward whom the ball is thrown. Another is what Americans call soccer, and the rest of world calls football, or *futbol*, which at least gets children running around outside until some blowhard know-it-all father (often from Europe) starts to set up zone offenses and offside traps which are pointless, because most American kids do not really care about soccer (or *futbol*). Nor should they.

Other popular American sports include basketball or swimming in the winter months, or of course, American football (rugby, but in full battle armor). The uniquely American way of adult-directed athletics assures the maximum number of sports-related injuries, which in turn, serves as a major contributor to the medical industrial complex, one of the most significant elements of the American economy. [33]

Besides economically helpful injury, youth sports as practiced in United States often lead to low self-esteem, further isolation of

---

[33]   While the rest of the world properly views medical expenses as dead weight to their economies, in an American economy based primarily on various forms of accounting fraud, such injuries that require expensive medical treatment are accounted for as if they *add* to the overall economy. This particular idiocy is one of the recurrent themes of this work.

already isolated children, and in the helpful case of some sports like ice hockey, frequent scuffles in the viewing stands and parking lots *among parents*. Those youths whose egos are not sufficiently damaged by their "youth sports" to keep playing them until at least the high school level, may in turn realize that their higher education aspirations may be far better served by being excellent athletes than they would be served by being good or even outstanding students. This is because, like everything else in the American context, the primary focus of institutions of higher learning is *money*, and it is believed that the richer alumni of said institutions write bigger checks when their favorite college sports teams are doing well.

Elite levels of college sport are, of course, highly successful businesses in their own right, often filling football stadiums with upwards of 100,000 fans, and some of them are even students from the colleges that are fielding the teams! In the truest American fashion, the business model of college sports is old school: *slavery*. Youth participating in major American college sports risk crippling injury for no pay, only for "athletic scholarships" to attend institutions where athletes often have horrendously poor rates of graduation. Still, because the elite of the college level have the potential to make the grade at the elite professional level, despite the long odds, the business model has proven surprisingly resilient to this day. Some elite college coaches have discovered an additional "side hustle" profit opportunity: the coaches *pretended* that favored students *who bribed them* were "recruited athletes," thus securing coveted admissions to elite academic institutions not otherwise available. [34]

At the elite professional levels, sport takes an unusual position in the American mindset, somewhere between the most popular form of entertainment and religion. Sport enthusiasts wearing the branded attire of their favorite clubs are a staple throughout the

---

[34]   McDonald, Scott, "College Admissions Scandal 2019: Everything We Know," *Newsweek* (Mar. 19, 2019) https://www.newsweek.com/college-admissions-scandal-2019-everything-we-know-1360969

world. In New York City on Sundays, such persons wear their attire not to the sporting event itself, but to bars that cater to other fans of the same team from another city wearing the same attire, be it a Cincinnati Bengals bar or Pittsburgh Steelers bar or (sigh) Dallas Cowboys bar. Football in the US is the major sporting outlet for viewing, just as *futbol* is in the rest of world. Only in the US, soccer never manages to climb any higher than fifth place among the big team sports.

Like global *futbol*, American football features 11 men a side. The 11 men in American football, however, don body armor, and the object of their game appears to be the infliction of spectacular injury on their opponents. Apparently, the popularity of American football took something of a hit recently when the President of United States complained of protests by some black players against police murders of black men, a staple of American "criminal justice," by kneeling during the playing of the American national anthem, itself a convoluted tribute to warmongering written by a slave owner. This appears to have taken many American fans by surprise, at least in the short term, when they discovered that most of the men wearing the colors of the teams that they support are actually black men. [35] Nonetheless, American football remains far more popular than all other sports in US. Things will surely work out. Any discussion of American football must center on the fact that its rulebook is substantially longer than the rulebooks of all other major American sports *combined*. Even youth football still must have several stripe-shirted referees trying to figure out the rules along the way often speaking to each other and the coaches as the game progresses. Each of several dozen "plays" initiated by each side starts in an orderly, programmed way, and then devolves into inevitable attempts to injure other players. Attempting to injure other players outside of the rules, however, will result in infractions, the penalty for which is

---

[35] Professional American football has a largely Black workforce. *See* Goodman, H.A., "70 Percent of NFL Players Are Black Men. Colin Kaepernick Should be Praised, Not Condemned," *HuffPost* (September 1, 2016) https://www.huffpost.com/entry/70-of-nfl-players-are-black-men-colin-kaepernick_b_57c7b12be4b07addc4114047

moving the ball one way or the other. Particular rules of American football are not really the point of this discussion; the fact that there are *so many rules* is.

Similarly, baseball, "the national pastime," is an entirely adjudicated game. In the professional ranks of baseball, one "umpire" lurks behind each of four bases, to make the appropriate adjudications more or less instantaneously.

The next most popular sports, basketball and ice hockey, are also adjudicated, but usually with fewer adjudicators, and in a manner more reminiscent of soccer, the games are more flowing, and most of the action does not require adjudication at all. Nonetheless, when the opinion of a referee is required, it is frequently considered to be arbitrary. Indeed, in both basketball and *futbol*, a key component of the game is called "the flop," where a player intentionally falls to the ground as theatrically as possible in an effort to get the referee to call a foul on another party. In *American* football, this would likely be called "unsportsmanlike conduct," but in basketball or soccer *futbol*, it is considered first-rate play, only if successful, of course. The aspect of American Exceptionalism associated with sports that we will discuss here is not the particular choice of sport. A number of Caribbean countries as well as Korea, Japan, and Taiwan excel at baseball, as well as at *futbol*. Canada, which of course, kicks ass in ice hockey, has its own version of *American* football, only, being Canada, it plays 12 men a side and features an even larger field than American football. Nonetheless, it appears to be the pitched combat in body armor (armour in Canada) where the object of the game seems to be infliction of injury. Much of the world plays a variation of this game called "rugby" that resembles American football, only without the body armor.

The American Exceptionalism angle in sport of relevance to our discussion is the singular American focus on the sports that obsess over rules and adjudications. No American football game could possibly be complete without several lengthy interruptions where referees go "under the hood" to review close calls that are challenged by one team or the other, or perhaps even by the referees themselves. Invariably, the lengthiest such interruptions take place during games played in northerly cities during winter months in outdoor stadiums. These stadiums seem to have been designed to inflict the maximum wind chill on spectators, who are evidently expected to be too inebriated from their automobile "tailgate parties" before the games to even notice the lengthy delays. Indeed, "bad calls" are such a serious matter, that sometimes American politicians seek to intervene on behalf of aggrieved sporting sides.

One of the leading American broadcasting formats is "sports talk radio." This format features perhaps two-to-three hours of an actual sporting event per day if that, and perhaps 21-22 hours per day of uninformed members of the public calling in to express their frustration with "bad calls." They also call to express their frustration with disfavored players, coaches, managers, owners, stadiums, mascots, cheerleaders, and so forth.

This concern with "fair play" and "bad calls" is also true of pretty much all American sports. Baseball is constantly adjudicated. It usually results in the fewest complaints, as baseball's professional referees are very good at their jobs, and as baseball umpires' decisions require less exercise of discretion than in the more "fluid" sports. Certainly, erroneous foul or penalty calls in basketball and hockey are also fodder for the ever discerning "first-time caller and long-time listener" who dominates the sports radio format, but football seems to be at a special level of concern. For one thing, the games are only once a week. In short, Americans are obsessed with "fairness" in their sport, and insist that the outcomes in sport must be "correct." They are, of course, less concerned when the "bad call" is in favor of their preferred team, but they are nonetheless concerned with the integrity of the game resulting in, perhaps, bad karma resulting in a "bad call" going against their own team at some future date. I cannot say it enough: Americans are gravely concerned with arbitrariness and unfairness in their sport.

I suggest that this is because virtually every aspect of American life besides sport—and organized sport at the higher levels at that—is replete with arbitrariness and unfairness. I do *not* suggest that arbitrariness and unfairness is in any way exceptional, or even that the United States excels in it more than other countries. Indeed, on the "corruption index," the US scores in the better half. It is hardly near the top, however, having recently fallen out of the top 20, and the US, alas, is now rated as a "flawed democracy." [36]

What I am suggesting is that the unusual American penchant for *legalism and litigation* and the daily risk that this puts on every aspect of every American's existence is staggering. The United States has a large number of lawyers: apparently over *1.3 million.* [37] You might think that this would make Americans the most law-obsessed and fairness-obsessed people on Earth, and that their courts would reflect this. In practice, the American legal system, like everything else in the American system, seems to be about money. The United States appears to have the best justice system money can buy. Hence, even mere middle-class, white people charged with crimes can often buy reasonable doubt for a reasonable fee with private attorneys. Few Americans will say this out loud; the judicial system still often polls as the most trusted branch of government. [38]

Nonetheless, as more Americans catch on to the judiciary's role as *the ultimate backstop of the powerful* against the rabble, even the judiciary's support may decline in its own right. [39]

Americans seem to know, intrinsically, that there is something "unfair" about a judicial system that incarcerates around 1% of its entire population at any given moment via its "criminal justice system." There could be something wrong in civil cases, as well, where courts almost invariably seem to rule in favor of the interests of the rich and the powerful. Of course, the United States

---

36   Karlis, Nicole, "New report classifies U.S. as a 'flawed democracy,' *Salon* (Jan. 31, 2018) https://www.salon.com/2018/01/31/new-report-classifies-us-as-a-flawed-democracy/
37   "Legal Profession Statistics," *American Bar Association* (May 31, 2019) https://www.americanbar.org/content/dam/aba/administrative/market_research/total-national-lawyer-population-1878-2019.pdf
38   Jones, Jeffrey M., "Trust in Judicial Branch Up, Executive Branch Down," *Gallup* (Sept. 20, 2017) https://news.gallup.com/poll/219674/trust-judicial-branch-executive-branch-down.aspx
39   *See* Jones, Jeffrey, "Trust in U.S. Judicial Branch Sinks to New Low of 53%," *Gallup* (Sept. 18, 2015) https://news.gallup.com/poll/185528/trust-judicial-branch-sinks-new-low.aspx

sports an economy where the powerful simply buy themselves subsidies or tax breaks or "freedom from regulation," while their competitors still have to compete; in this environment, the courts are considered an oasis of fairness. But even in the "adjudicated" sphere of American life, there is a growing perception that someone's thumb seems to be on the scale.

Where were we? Oh, yes. Given the perceived unfairness of the overall functioning of American society, is it any wonder that fairness *in sport* is so important in American consciousness? In American life, and indeed, as a true matter of American Exceptionalism, sports are one of the few areas where Americans actually *expect* "truth and justice."

Interestingly, entertainment is another.

5. That's Entertainment

WHILE SPORT IS ONE OF the more prominent entertainment avenues particularly enjoyed by American men (there are many women fans, too, of course), the Hollywood dream factory also provides *other* media for the "enjoyment" of all. Thus, Hollywood produces entertainment that results in passive viewing by a vast army of American zombies through its movies, television programs, video games, music, and, since the same media conglomerates often own book publishing enterprises, what passes for literature. Its products are essential to any thorough discussion of American Exceptionalism. It was Oscar Wilde who said, "The good ended happily, and the bad unhappily. That is what Fiction means." The "happy ending" is, of course, the "cover story" for American life, and no one is better at putting out cover stories than the Hollywood dream factory. While both literature and live stage theatre have long American traditions, American Exceptionalism in the field of entertainment really exploded as it were once filmed pictures started moving. Indeed, famous *American* anti-Semite Thomas Edison is credited with inventing the moving picture camera and projector in the late 19th century. Many of the film masters in the early days of the medium were, of course, *Americans*.

One of the "landmark" early films was a brilliant piece of filmmaking by motion picture pioneer D.W. Griffith. It was also a vile propaganda piece. The film was called *Birth of a Nation*. [40]

The film lauded white supremacy and the Ku Klux Klan during the so-called Reconstruction period following the American Civil War. [41] Although stories of American racism can and do fill many volumes, we reference *Birth of a Nation* here because it is a useful demonstration of the power of storytelling. Indeed, competent storytelling has always been essential for manipulating the American public to maintain its continued belief in the underpinnings of American Exceptionalism. The key to the exercise is the establishment of "good guys" to *root for;* amazingly, members of the Ku Klux Klan were designated *the good guys* in *Birth of a Nation*. Once the "good guys" are established, we then identify the "bad guys." In *Birth of a Nation*, these are opportunistic northern aggressors, the "carpetbaggers". Then we *root against them.* Simple as that. Reality outside the context of the story itself is irrelevant.

Of course, American cinema moved in other directions besides pro-southern propaganda. American cinema also celebrated the joys of massacring native peoples in the genre called "westerns." To be sure, the western genre was also very helpful in maintaining the overall white supremacy racial narrative complete with white hats being "the good guys" and black hats being "the bad guys." Still, westerns proved even better at advancing the other American founding narrative of "rugged individualism" than almost any other genre. In a typical western, we overlook the fact that white townspeople have to rely on each other as well as *the American military* for help. In particular, such help is needed to suppress any indigenous persons who had survived earlier rounds of disease or genocide who might still have grievances. In other times, such an

---

40   Clark, Alexis, "How 'The Birth of a Nation' Revived the Ku Klux Klan," *History* (Mar. 11, 2019) https://www.history.com/news/kkk-birth-of-a-nation-film
41   The Civil War is yet another demonstration of American Exceptionalism. A struggle of industrial power versus agrarian society of that kind would ordinarily serve to end feudalism and move the impacted nation on the full path to modern industrial development. As usual, however, American Exceptionalism prevailed, and formal chattel slavery was replaced by the less formal proto-slavery called "sharecropping" in large parts of the American South. Further, the tightly racist social order of the slavery system was replaced by "Jim Crow laws," which served to ensure that post-Civil War Constitutional promises of racial equality in the Thirteenth, Fourteenth, and Fifteenth Amendments did not change the "facts on the ground" in the American South.

obligation of mutual defense from the feudal lords to the peasants would be considered part of "the social contract." In the western, this all plays out amidst the vast backdrop of the open West (actually, studios and constructed sets in metropolitan Los Angeles, for the most part).

American audiences absorbed good vs. evil dramas on a scale that they could understand. Such spectacles eliminated the irritating subtlety or ambiguity that they had to deal with in their ordinary lives. Other genres of film, crime drama, screwball comedy, and musicals, for example, also featured simplistic stories which were thoroughly resolved in an hour and a half to two hours. These films enabled the American audience to leave the theater singing and smiling, after witnessing the mainstay of American storytelling, the "happy ending." Concepts from American cinema and American theater translated easily into the early broadcast medium of radio, and its close relative, television. Whereas ticket buyers paid for cinema and now, more and more television viewers pay for subscriptions to see their favorite channels, as well as for all forms of cable television, early American broadcast radio and television went for a crass advertising-based model. [42]

Early variations of this form of air pollution included entire sponsorships of popular programs. Eventually the 30- or 60-second commercial message became the standard, and now, in the 21st century, virtually all forms of media including paid cinema and paid cable or satellite television remain infested with this obnoxious waste product. The commercial advert is intended to both capture American consciousness *and as a bonus* to reinforce the message that Americans are intrinsically worthless and can only buy momentary ego satisfaction by consuming the advertised product.

One of the great early pioneers in this area was one Edward Bernays, no relation to the differently spelled sauce; in fact, Bernays was Sigmund Freud's nephew. Bernays pioneered the concept of

---

42   *See, e.g.* White, Thomas, "United States Early Radio History, Section 20," *Financing Radio Broadcasting* (retrieved June 7, 2019) http://earlyradiohistory.us/sec020.htm

"engineered consent," and, for his service to American capitalism, earned the title "the father of public relations." [43]

Bernays's greatest coup, according to most observers, was getting women marchers in New York City's famous Easter Parade no less to smoke cigarettes during this event. He managed to pitch their cigarettes as "liberty torches," *i.e.*, women were now "free" (you have to admire Americans' sense of humor) to support corporate America by consuming a carcinogenic and expensive product. The brilliant gambit worked, as women dramatically increased their consumption of cigarettes, a bullish event for that product and for the influence of advertising, branding, and its companion disciplines. In due course, on-the-air advertising pollution also infested the political system, where hyperbole and bunk were always currency of the realm, and "the political commercial" came to dominate the airwaves in the latter part of the 20th century and early 21st as any election approached.

Commercials came to dominate all forms of American "entertainment," because for the most part, advertising revenue from these commercials ultimately pays for the outsized compensation packages of the entertainment personalities or "celebrities" who are worshipped as gods in the American context. Indeed, on many television programs, it is often quite hard to ascertain whether commercial advertising or the programming itself will take more of the viewing slot's allotted time. Worse, it is hard to tell whether the commercial advertising or the programming is more entertaining. This phenomenon became more acute with the unfortunate rise of a particularly awful form of television programming called "reality television," which is a long-form version of the popular game show format. The difference between a reality show and a game show is that a game show invariably involves some skill, whether answering trivia questions or performing some act of physical skill, or for some

---

43   "Edward Bernays, 'Father of Public Relations' And Leader in Opinion Making, Dies at 103," *New York Times* (March 10, 1995) https://archive.nytimes.com/www.nytimes.com/books/98/08/16/specials/bernays-obit.html

of the more asinine and hence, more popular game shows, just being the *luckiest* person in the room. Reality television is the platform from which a failed local New York confidence man named Donald Trump magically became a world-class businessman in need of an "apprentice." Reality television arose most prominently at the same time that American scripted drama was suffering an existential crisis on network television because unionized writers were actually demanding fair and appropriate compensation, never a good move in American labor/management relations. [44] Fortunately, the writers' union was crushed. Nonetheless, scripted dramas are back, albeit mostly on the paid-for "cable" channels. Unfortunately, the writers' strike also created an opening for "reality television," where the narrative was created not in a unionized writer's room, but in the non-unionized editing room.

In the world of television game shows, "competition" plays out among contestants engaged in games of skill. On *Survivor,* the leading program of the genre stolen from a Swedish concept by the same former British military paratrooper who eventually blessed us with *The Apprentice,* the contestants engage in games that include feats of physical prowess or daring: winning sack races, eating the most parasite-ridden bugs, or whatever. Prevailing in these contests, however, does not appear to be the object of the game. Rather, the contestants dutifully express their gripes about their fellow contestants to a conveniently located camera, and a duly constructed narrative is provided to the audience. Contestants are then adjudicated not on their skill or even on the entertainment value of their contributions to the narrative, but instead, on the most arbitrary of criteria. Specifically, such contestants are adjudged either by clueless idiots designated to exercise authority such as Mr. Trump, whose only qualification to wield power was that the producers of the show assigned it to him, or possibly by the only thing worse, the votes of *their fellow contestants*! The irony is that this format has proven insanely successful because of the use of such subjective and arbitrary criteria, which seems to mirror *exactly*

44   *See* Grant, Drew, "10 year time capsule: When reality TV took over," *Salon.com* (April 26, 2011) https://www.salon.com/2011/04/26/10_year_time_capsule_writers_strike/

how most employees are evaluated in the American work place! Such arbitrary work-place decisions, of course, lead to decisions on compensation, or whether employees even get to work at all, and hence, have health care, food, shelter, self-esteem, etc. An actual *healthy* person might think that this is horrifying and change the channel. [45]

Because comparatively few Americans are healthy in any category of their lives, "reality television" programs have been the breakout success of the 21st century! "The tribe has spoken" or "you're fired," respectively the catch phrases from *Survivor* and *The Apprentice*, have become cultural icons in their own right.

My own theory is that the last semblance of self-esteem for the overwhelming majority of American population was destroyed by the late-20th century. This coincided, at least temporally, with one of the greatest empty political slogans of all time well before "Hope and Change" and "Make America Great Again" perfected the art of empty political slogans in this century. Specifically, I am referring to Bill Clinton's slogan, "Build a bridge to the 21st century." It was not without irony that just eight years into the 21st century, a leading Republican candidate, Alaska Governor Sarah Palin, was famous for supposedly *opposing* a bridge, the infamous "Bridge to Nowhere." [46]

With an audience now devoid of self-esteem that wants to see abuses similar to those regularly meted out in the American workplace piled onto hapless "contestants," reality television's singular form of visual torture has become one of the most successful entertainment genres ever. It has spawned such other atrocities as real housewives of various cliché places such as New Jersey or

---

45   A great deal of the success of American game shows is their relative *lack* of arbitrariness: as in American sport, fastidious adherence to codes of conduct is essential, lest the American head proverbially explode from the "unfairness," as it did during the famous "Quiz Show Scandals" of the 1950s.

46   In Governor Palin's case, it was not clear at what point in time she opposed this particular boondoggle for her low-population state that was secured by its effective U.S. Senator, Ted Stevens. *See* Hornick, Ed, "Stevens' Senate career hurt by 'bridge to nowhere,'" *CNN* (July 29, 2008) http://www.cnn.com/2008/POLITICS/07/29/stevens.history/ The bridge was not exactly to nowhere, but from a small island near Ketchikan, Alaska, where that town's airport was located, to the larger island on which the town was located. It was, of course, an expensive project with few actual users, but "bridge to nowhere" is still a cool name. Let's face it, as a metaphor for life in the "Exceptional" American 21st century, it could not be more perfect.

Beverly Hills, or the *Shahs of Sunset*, or a seemingly infinite number of disagreeable people named Kardashian, or incredibly irritating people who are forced to stay together in the same *Big Brother* house. Regardless of the reason, and it cannot be a good reason, these and so many other "reality television programs" have come to infest the viewing habits of an amazingly large number of Americans. Thus, as we consider the state of American entertainment from the standpoint of American Exceptionalism, where the highest value is being famous for no other reason than being famous, we must extend props to the television arm of the Hollywood dream factory. The format has managed to get non-professional actors to show up and just be themselves and "compete" in order to be treated arbitrarily and abusively for no reason other than the entertainment of the rest of us! While they do this, of course, highly profitable commercial advertising is presented several times per hour!

Another staple of American entertainment is "the video game." This is another of the most successful genres of "entertainment." It gives people who have no job prospects whatsoever whether because of a pointlessly expensive and time-consuming but still useless "education," or simply because they have had their self-esteem, and possibly their physical health, destroyed by the American system something to do during their waking hours, especially when their favorite television shows are not on. While there are an almost infinite variety of such games, popular entrees include "Doom," "Grand Theft Auto," "Mortal Kombat," or an otherwise infinite number of opportunities to engage in virtual violence. Of course, once one is tired of television or video games, the Internet has also provided wonderful opportunities for entertainment. The two most profitable services offered on the Internet, of course, remain pornography and gambling.

Ever thus.

6. WORKING 9 TO 5 (OR AT ALL)

AMERICAN LABOR AND WORK conditions are *so* exceptional that we will return to them many times. The basic premise is quite simple, and it is always the same: American employers will extract the maximum value that they can from their labor force, while compensating and usually treating their labor force as miserably as possible. American free-market orthodoxy, or more accurately, free market Stalinism, is well-ingrained in nearly all Americans. This orthodoxy includes the belief that others want to come to the United States for its glorious economic and political system, rather than simply because the American empire has sucked all the value out of the rest of the planet and in its place installed political unrest, death squads, and toxic waste. Fortunately, most Americans are not particularly well-informed about how their own working and living conditions measure up against those of the rest of the world. For the most part, Americans are not well-versed about the *existence* of the rest of the world. American Exceptionalism in labor practices is embedded in the American consciousness at a molecular level. I suspect that the hatred for labor unions among American capitalists may even be at a *sub-atomic* level! From the organization of work and why it is so meaningless and even painful for most Americans, to the work environment, to compensation (why Americans, uniquely, get "a la carte" compensation and "fringe benefits" that are so expensive to the employer, but often so valueless to the employee), to "the default contract" among American workers ("employment at will" as is practiced in the US is almost unique in the world), American labor practices are truly exceptional.

It is not without irony that American law books discuss the employment relationship under the indexed term "master and servant." The default American work relationship unless you work for yourself or your family remains ostensible slavery. By one observation, the United States is one of only ten countries with "employment at will." [47] Even this is a bit of an overstatement, since of these ten, Brunei Darussalam, Israel, the Marshall Islands, Micronesia, Myanmar, Palau, Papua New Guinea, Tonga, the United States, and Uruguay, four of them, the United States itself, the Marshall Islands, Micronesia, and Palau, are essentially American military protectorates, complete with American zip codes. The official justifying reason for why the "master" in the employment relationship can sack the "servant" at any moment is that the "servant" can quit working for the "master" at any time. However, this is capitalist, self-serving tautological nonsense. "Slavery," the official condition by which the servant *can't* quit work for the master, is *officially against the law* in every country on Earth. A glaring exception to this official outlawing of slavery is, of course, widely practiced within the United States itself! Specifically, the Thirteenth Amendment to the United States Constitution provides:

Neither slavery nor involuntary servitude, except as a punishment for crime whereof the party shall have been duly convicted, shall exist within the United States, or any place subject to their jurisdiction.

That middle part, about "except as a punishment for crime whereof the party shall have been duly convicted" takes on an interesting

47   Sillers, Don, "What Countries in the World Don't Have At Will Employment?" *Quora. com* (March 10, 2016)   https://www.quora.com/What-countries-in-the-world-dont-have-at-will-employment. The commentator observes that the World Bank criteria for employment at will are met by these countries because "In those ten countries, there is no maximum probationary period for a new employee; employees can be dismissed without prior notification to, or approval by third parties; no requirements for training or reassignment of dismissed workers; no priority rules for redundancies; and no priority rules for reemployment."

connotation in a country that incarcerates more human beings than any other country or empire in the history of the world, an estimated two-to-three *million* at any one time. Indeed, noted law professor and researcher Michelle Alexander has observed that as of the early part of the 21st century, there were more black men incarcerated in "penal servitude" in the United States than there had been enslaved in chattel slavery in the 1850s. [48]

Aside from performing the kind of tasks you would expect of such prisoners, such as work within the prison (laundries, kitchens, painting, and so forth), or even services to the state that incarcerates them, famously making license plates, for example, prisoners' involuntary labor (the prisoners are often "paid," although typically at the rate of one dollar per day *or less*) is often farmed out. [49] Sometimes, prisoners' labor is even farmed out to actual farms, a/k/a "American agri-business," another example of American Exceptionalism. Indeed, such "involuntary servitude" is often exploited for the benefit of some of the largest and most-profitable business corporations on Earth. It is hardly a coincidence that American mega-corporations can be extremely profitable when their labor costs are perilously close to non-existent, thanks in part to the prison industrial complex.

It is not without irony (everything about American Exception-alism has a healthy serving of irony) that working-class, white peo-ple tend to be so supportive of overtly racist measures like the "war on drugs." [50] Make no mistake: they support such measures *be-cause* they are overtly racist, even though their ultimate effect is to ensnare many poor white people into the penal system. The penal system, in turn, is replete with arbitrary junk fees and ridiculously arbitrary rules that result in the system being essentially inescap-

48   Lu, Thoai, "Michelle Alexander: More Black Men in Prison Than Were Enslaved in 1850," *ColorLines* (March 30, 2011) https://www.colorlines.com/articles/michelle-alexander-more-black-men-prison-were-enslaved-1850

49   "Prison labour is a billion-dollar industry, with uncertain returns for inmates," *The Economist* (March 16, 2017) https://www.economist.com/united-states/2017/03/16/prison-labour-is-a-billion-dollar-industry-with-uncertain-returns-for-inmates

50   "Race and the Drug War," *DrugPolicy.Org* (retrieved June 7, 2019) http://www.drugpolicy.org/issues/race-and-drug-war

able for the short-of-cash. Also ironic is that other than the relatively modest although geographically well-placed job opportunities for corrections officers and others staffing the prisons, working-class, white people simply cannot compete with *slave* labor, even at the outrageously low American minimum wage. [51]

Indeed, over the last 50 years, the forces of globalization and neo-liberalism, or more accurately "sado-monetarism," as well as technological "improvements," have enabled workers in other parts of the globe (hence "globalization") to compete directly against the American working class. Of course, all of this occurred at the precise moment when the capitalists had finally succeeded in the destruction of the American union movement. Studies strongly suggest that the decline in union membership has had a serious negative effect, even on non-unionized workers. [52]

Nonetheless, even though American wages for the bulk of workers have been flat or actually declining in real terms, [53] they have still not gone down nearly enough to compete with proper slave labor, whether in Latin America, which at least has the virtue of relative proximity, or with Eastern, Southern, and Central Asia, or to a growing extent, with Africa, or wherever on Earth genuinely low-wage, low-overhead labor conditions can be repeated. Of course, as the so-called "developing world" increases its own standard of living, its wages eventually rise in real terms. Nonetheless, the magical forces of the "free market" have meant that if a job can be "outsourced" to a lower cost venue, it generally will be or has been already. This leads our discussion to the other large stone piled on to the back of the American worker. This is not, of course, competition from "undocumented" or "illegal alien" workers, who

51   If the minimum wage were inflation adjusted over the last 50 years, the minimum wage would be over $20 per hour, instead of the well under $10 per hour it is now. *See* Babones, Salvatore, "The Minimum Wage is Stuck at $7.25; It Should be $21.16 – or Higher," *Inequality.Org*, (July 24, 2012) https://inequality.org/research/minimum-wage/
52   Davidson, Paul, "Decline of unions has hurt all workers: study," *USA Today* (Sep. 5, 2016) https://www.usatoday.com/story/money/2016/08/30/decline-unions-has-hurt-all-workers-study/89557266/
53   Stein, Jeff and Van Dam, Andrew, "For the biggest group of American workers, wages aren't just flat. They're Falling." *Washington Post* (June 15, 2018) http://cc.bingj.com/cache.aspx?q=for+most+american+workers+wages+declining&d=4684458317972455&mkt=en-US&setlang=en-US&w=CKoRYlYFbA1SPrF82FNU_3WMNm6nrnmp

generally tend to perform back-breaking agricultural, food service, or construction work at insanely low pay that American workers really (seriously) don't want to do. No, I am talking about that primary driver of "progress" that causes so much wonderful human misery: automation. Automation is the logical omega point for so many American job functions, particularly in the manufacturing realm. The original methods that resulted in so many manufacturing tasks being so easily transferred over to machines were first dictated by the Bonnie and Clyde of capitalist ergonomics, Frank and Lillian Gilbreth. [54] Similar work in the field of advancing human misery by making work "efficient" for the capitalists rather than *in any way* joyful or meaningful for the workers actually *performing it* was undertaken by Frederick Taylor. [55]

If you have heard of the Gilbreths at all, it is likely from their tale of supposedly hilarious neglect of their *own* children called *Cheaper by the Dozen*. Whether you have heard of them or not, they have been responsible for at least a century of untold human misery through their horrifying efforts to make work more "efficient" by turning human beings into machines in the name of "efficiency." As a result, humans performing repetitive tasks could perform far more of them in any given period of time. As hourly wage is based on hours worked, this *presumably* meant that it in any given period of time, more units of *whatever* could be generated by the same number of worker hours, and this is the key, *without paying the workers any more*. If workers developed horrifying injuries as a result of the repetition or perhaps, quite literally, *went insane*, this was just too damned bad. The country was awash in immigrants and their children who could serve as cannon fodder for the American industrial army. In the early and especially middle parts of the 20th century, American manufacturing also had the benefit of internal immigrants fleeing southern sharecropping and Jim Crow laws, not

---

54   *See* Caramela, Sammi, "The Management Theory of Frank and Lillian Gilbreth," *Business. com* (Feb. 26, 2018) https://www.business.com/articles/management-theory-of-frank-and-lillian-gilbreth/
55   *See* Caramela, Sammi, "The Management Theory of Frederick Taylor," *Business.com* (Feb. 11, 2019) https://www.business.com/articles/management-theory-of-frederick-taylor/

to mention an agricultural sector that was itself in the process of industrializing.

Hence, decades of repetitive stress injury and/or sheer madness were underway among American workers, all in the name of increasing profit.

Fortunately for the capitalists, as the 20th century wore on, the United States managed to come out of the Second World War as the only relatively unscathed major industrial power. Thus, it could dictate political and military terms to the rest of world, except for the Soviet bloc, always a thorn in the side of the American imperial system. From this position of extreme strength, American industrialists found that they could dictate the prices and terms of raw materials supplied to them, and prices of industrial products they sold to the rest of world. This, of course, is an excellent position from which to maintain economic hegemony. And fortunately, this also included the ability to dictate the price of energy, particularly oil. The US has always been among the world's largest producers of oil in its own right.

Eventually, the rebuilt industrial powers of Europe, especially Germany, needed oil. So did Japan. Their oil came largely from the Middle East, and this oil was supplied largely on American terms and priced and payable in American dollars. Oil has always been insanely underpriced compared to the fact that it is a dwindling resource; once extracted, it cannot be replaced. The use of oil also usually results in *highly toxic* "externalities." With a big assist from the Pentagon, oil remains ridiculously underpriced to this very day. [56] As the 19th century faded further into the past and the 20th century and its industrial-scale genocides wore on, ever more functions once performed by human or animal muscle instead were performed by machines. These machines usually operated on burned coal or

---

56   Issues of petroleum's stranglehold control on the American system (the Rockefeller family, for example, famously controlled key levers of *both* oil and money) present an amazing tale of American Exceptionalism in its own right. You might well be asking why we are discussing oil in the context of the exploitation of American *labor*. The best answer is that neither "oligarchy" nor "oligopoly" can be properly spelled without the letters O, I and L.

petroleum. Although some industrial functions might have been performed with the help of falling water, as, presumably a waterfall is "renewable," this could only be done in a finite number of places. If capital had to go in search of labor in select locations where labor might be able to dictate terms and wages, then capital might not be able to impose slavery-like conditions. [57]

Fortunately, fossil fuel was widely located, and in any event, could easily be transported to where capital could best exploit labor surpluses rather than have *labor* exploit labor shortages for its own benefit. Hence, labor found its rightful place as a human cog in a vast industrial machine. As the 20th century wore on, conditions for the mass of American labor actually improved in a very real sense, perhaps for the only time, ever, after the unfortunate set-backs associated with "the Great Depression." At the time, of course, the Second World War left the United States as the only major industrial power still standing. And at that very moment, the US had also succeeded in maximizing its domestic petroleum production, resulting in plentiful, relatively inexpensive, energy sources.

As if things were not already good enough for the American worker, who had long enjoyed the default American labor arrangement, ostensible slavery, some of the Progressive and New Deal-era reforms such as limited hour workweeks, limitations on child labor, workers' compensation programs for workplace injuries, etc. were ramping up as well. These measures were aided by a robust union movement which, synergistically, also benefited from support in the Roosevelt Administration and Congress at the time. [58]

At this heady time, perhaps because of fear of socialist movements that gained traction in the 1930s and perhaps out of fear of the "Red Menace" in the 1940s and '50s, the denizens of the

---

57   *See* Malm, Andreas, "The Origins of Fossil Capital: From Water to Steam in the British Cotton Industry," *Historical Materialism 21.,1* at 15–68 (2013) https://geosci.uchicago.edu/~moyer/GEOS24705/Readings/From_water_to_steam.pdf
58   *See e.g.*, "Great Depression and World War II, 1929-1945, *Library of Congress Teachers Presentation and Activities* (retrieved June 7, 2019) http://loc.gov/teachers/classroommaterials/presentationsandactivities/presentations/timeline/depwwii/unions/

American industrial system seemed to believe that they needed to compete with Soviet Russia and its communistic system. [59]

Post-World War II America improved the lot of its working people (mostly men) with an unprecedented, seen never before and seen never since blowout expansion of wages and living standards for the ordinary American worker. This included expansion of opportunities for the children of said American workers to get first-rate educations, and even to move from the working class into the middle and even the upper-middle class.

All of this advancement of the American worker took place with the fundamental default, norm institutions of ostensible slavery still in place: employment at will, employer-paid health care, only if the employer felt like providing it, no mandatory child care or maternity benefits, no mandatory retirement plans, no mandatory paid vacations, etc. Nonetheless, for the first time, and as it would turn out, the last time in American history, most workers in both the private and public sectors could reasonably expect their employer to provide them with employer-paid health care, paid vacations, and some kind of employer-paid pension or retirement plan *on top of a living wage.* This wage, paid to a single, usually male, worker, could successfully support *an entire household.* Even a working-class family could afford a freestanding suburban house, one or more automobiles, and most accoutrements of middle-class life, including the ability to travel on vacations, higher education for the children, and health care that would not result in personal financial ruination. The family would even have the comfort level of knowing that a non-terminal illness, or perhaps a vehicular or home maintenance mishap would not also result in their financial destruction.

Because both parents were not required to work under this dispensation, many of the uniquely vicious American cruelties

---

[59]   The Soviet system operated a much less prosperous consumer economy than the United States, and it was, of course, a totalitarian regime. Nonetheless, the USSR still managed to provide virtually all of its citizens with housing, education, health care, jobs, public transport, and, at least most of the time, food. (For good measure, the USSR also managed to win the first several laps of the "space race.")

associated with the refusal to provide paid maternity leave or child care or even to make appropriate allowances for them were resolved by paying sufficient wages to "the man of the house." As a default model, ably depicted on virtually all television programs from the 1940s and '50s through the 1980s, if not even later, men would leave the home for work, and "home-making" women remained in a position to provide child care within the home. In those cases where the woman also left the home to work, the couple's combined salaries were more than sufficient to afford household servants. Where there were children, but only one parent, in most cases, a female parent, the usual result was, as it still is, poverty. Then, by the mid to late 1970s, the two or three decades of American workers' paradise associated with the post-War era began to come apart. While the default American labor arrangement, still modeled on slavery, never really disappeared, its intrinsic viciousness became more acute as women entered the work force in the millions by the 1980s. It is hard to pinpoint exactly what brought about this change in macro-conditions, but part of the sudden reversal was caused by oil price shocks. The most notable of these oil shocks, the 1973 Arab oil embargo, arose in response to American support of Israel during the 1973 Yom Kippur War. A second major oil shock stemmed from the 1979 Iranian revolution resulting in disruption of supply from the Persian Gulf. As a result, the US removed many of its oil-price controls by the late 1970s, in turn resulting in higher prices for oil. This, in turn, resulted in higher-input prices for industrial production, as well as higher costs to consumers for gasoline, heating fuel, and everything transported via diesel-fuel burning trucks, *i.e.,* *everything*.

Part of the reversal was likely caused by the eventual reckoning associated with the accumulation of various deficits resulting from the conduct of the Vietnam War. These trade and "current account" deficits resulted in net outflows of American capital often in the form of gold bullion, and by the early 1970s, the outflows were so severe that the US officially withdrew from its last ties to the international gold standard.

Against this backdrop of 1970's economic decline of so-called "stagflation" and "malaise" that interestingly coincided with a rather vibrant period in American culture, particularly in music and cinema, the 1980s arrived. By the end of the first year of that decade, Ronald Reagan, the ultimate avatar of free-market Stalinism and sado-monetarist policies, was elected as the 40th President of the United States with the promise of the restoration of an American working-class cornucopia.   Did he ever deliver! Reagan saw that greed was good! The American industrial slowdown of the 1970s ended, and industrial output roared back to life. Unemployment went down, and the American living-standard cornucopia resumed. For good measure, the United States eventually spent the Soviet Union into oblivion, winning the Cold War, or so goes the story.

Only decades later did Americans notice that the Reagan-era prosperity was largely illusory. Indeed, the "prosperity" was not so much the result of growth as it was on many Americans accumulating outrageously high levels of debt. The significantly lowered income taxes ushered in by Reagan resulted in ever-increasing governmental structural deficits even as rising Social Security payroll tax increased, this regressive tax possibly causing many women to have to enter the workforce as take-home pay for single-earner males declined. Vast volumes of tax revenue once associated with maintaining social safety nets went uncollected, so that the money remained in the pockets of the richest oligarchs. The oligarchs, in turn, used their increased capital to procure the favors of members of Congress to increase their own capital, yet further, always at the expense of everyone else.

Of course, the default American working arrangement largely reverted to the norm, as the 1980s and 1990s wore on, and as more women entered the work force. The unique features of American working life such as no mandatory paid vacation, maternity leave or child care, health care, etc. remained in place, only now in two-working-parent families.

In the kind of propaganda coup that Americans excel at, another area of American Exceptionalism, the declining real wages and other conditions that forced millions of women to work outside the home and abandon their children to strangers was pitched as "women's liberation." Edward Bernays himself would have been proud of the framing! The depressing reality was that millions of women joined a working life that not only defaulted to the usual American arrangement, a one-way feudal obligation of ostensible slavery, but women were and still are usually paid significantly less than men for performing similar work, if not the same job. [60]

Nearing the end of the second decade of the 21st century and decades after Reagan, still sainted in right-wing circles, wages have continued to decline precipitously in real terms, while debt at every level—personal, educational, business, government—has exploded. Working Americans find themselves incurring ever more debt just to maintain their pre-existing living standards.

We come full circle, as debt has always been the basis of indenture in the American system. The great question for Americans at this point in their history is what happens when a fundamentally flawed labor-management and attendant social services system, the worst in the developed world in many ways and the worst *in the entire world* in some ways, can no longer paper over its shortcomings through spectacular growth and rapidly improving living standards. In fact, not only is growth lacking, but for all but the upper strata of American society, real living standards are actually *declining*. Perhaps the answer, as the old American joke suggests, is that life sucks, and then you die, if you are lucky.

We consider that possibility in the next chapter.

---

60   Webb, Jonathan, "Women Are Still Paid Less Than Men - Even In The Same Job," *Forbes. Com* (March, 31, 2016) https://www.forbes.com/sites/jwebb/2016/03/31/women-are-still-paid-less-than-men-even-in-the-same-job/

7. DEATH AND/OR TAXES

I N AMERICAN LIFE, IT is said that nothing is certain except death and taxes; early American polymath, Benjamin Franklin, gets the attribution for that. In the case of taxes, this is not usually a problem, either for very poor Americans or for very rich ones, because neither group tends to pay much or sometimes *any* tax at all. [61]

Most taxes in the American context are paid by people in a certain "sweet spot." These people earn enough income to actually have the money to pay tax, but they do not have *so much* income or so much *wealth* that they can purchase the favors of national and state legislators to decree by law that the particular category of *their own income* is magically beyond taxation. A class of super rich can arrange to legislate away much of their own tax obligation because of the brute power to do so in a "democracy" that is actually for sale to the highest bidder. To be sure, these people are simply taking advantage of the engineered stupidity of the American people. By way of example, one of the fairest and most efficient taxes ever conceived is the estate tax. Nothing could be fairer than a tax upon people who clearly have no further use for their money: *the dead*. Of course, the fair and efficient estate tax has instead become "the death tax," duly pitched as the vilest concoction any misguided legislature

---

61 "Fact Sheet: Taxing Wealthy Americans," *Americans for Tax Fairness*, (retrieved June 7, 2019) https://americansfortaxfairness.org/tax-fairness-briefing-booklet/fact-sheet-taxing-wealthy-americans/

ever created. [62] Hence, in the American imagination, a "death tax"
only paid by fabulously rich people, is a horror story to be avoided at
all cost while it remains perfectly reasonable to *tax homeless people*
on *their* immense earnings. Death is somewhat less avoidable than
taxation. Although the rich and powerful do seemingly manage to
live almost forever; banking magnate and oil scion David Rockefeller
finally succumbed at age 101; Warren Buffett seems older than that,
and we seem to have stopped counting how old Henry Kissinger
is. The harsh reality is that the oligarchs have not quite obtained
immortality through their money although they are continually
trying. For Americans as a whole, used to paying for the world's most
expensive "health care," death is a little too familiar. American life
expectancy clocks in at just under 79, well below the OECD average,
[63] and indeed, a "nothing to write home about" placing of 34th or so
in world rankings. [64]

We will come back to this subject, given some of the absurd ways
in which Americans die to a degree that can only be termed "American
Exceptionalism." These include gun violence, medical mistakes, [65]
automobile accidents, and post-childbirth maternal mortality, just
to name a few avoidable causes of death that a "leading First World
nation" should have moved past long ago. First, we toggle back
to taxes. We take a brief diversion into one area where American
Exceptionalism is *truly* exceptional, that of expatriate taxation, a field
which the United States has all to itself, except for Eritrea, which for
some reason insists on a whopping 2% tax on its expatriate citizens,

---

62   *See* Lessenberry, Jack, "The great death tax lie," *Detroit MetroTimes* (October 18,
2017) https://www.metrotimes.com/detroit/the-great-death-tax-lie/Content?oid=6343655
63   Donnelly, Grace, "Here's Why Life Expectancy in the U.S. Dropped Again This Year,"
Fortune.com (Feb. 9, 2018) http://fortune.com/2018/02/09/us-life-expectancy-dropped-again/
64   "United States Life Expectancy," *World Health Rankings* (accessed June 6, 2019) https://
www.worldlifeexpectancy.com/united-states-life-expectancy
65   Sipherd, Ray, "The third-leading cause of death in US most doctors don't want you to know
about," *CNBC.com* (Feb. 28. 2018) https://www.cnbc.com/2018/02/22/medical-errors-third-leading-
cause-of-death-in-america.html. It is possible that the category of medical mistake might also include
medication-related deaths, some from prescribing or administering mistakes, some from abuse, and
some just from the unavoidable realities of how many medications work.

for which it has been almost universally criticized. [66] The United States, by contrast, imposes its regular full taxation obligations on all of its citizens, regardless of where on Earth they may be, except, for some reason, if they are in the American colony of Puerto Rico. Regular American taxation obligations for citizens can be as high as 39-1/2% of income plus whatever certain states and municipalities might try to pile on top of that. Unlike Eritrea, which has a hard-enough time implementing and executing its taxation laws *within Eritrea*, the mighty United States of America, commander of the world's reserve currency and possessor of the power to cut off other nations' ability to access international banking, has little problem convincing most other countries of the world to play along and cooperate in soaking its expatriate citizens. It is small wonder that Americans are renouncing their vaunted American citizenship at record rates. [67]

Of course, while Americans think that they are insanely burdened by tax, this type of self-aggrandizing misperception is yet another area of American Exceptionalism. The average rate of taxation, in *real* terms, government spending as against GDP in OECD countries, is about 33%; it is only about 26% in the US. [68] And despite the belief of the insane complexity of the American tax code, the United States only ranks 55th in "complexity of compliance." [69]

To be sure, there are substantial local and regional differences within the United States with respect to tax rates and tax complexity. Nonetheless, those below the 50th percentile in income pay comparatively little tax, a result of a combination of lower earnings and much lower progressive tax rates on their lower earnings. [70]

66   Giambruno, Nick, "Only Two Countries Do This Appalling Thing – And the U.S. Is One of Them," *Doug Casey's International Man* (retrieved June 6, 2019) https://internationalman.com/articles/this-appalling-practice-is-only-used-in-two-nations-and-the-us-is-one-of-th/
67   Morris, Chris, "Americans Are Ditching Their U.S. Citizenship at a Record Rate," *Fortune* (Nov. 6, 2017) http://fortune.com/2017/11/06/americans-renouncing-u-s-citizenship/
68   "How do US taxes compare internationally?," *The Tax Policy Center's Briefing Book* (retrieved June 6, 2019) https://www.taxpolicycenter.org/briefing-book/how-do-us-taxes-compare-internationally
69   Pomerlau, Kyle, "It Takes 175 hours for a U.S. Business to Comply with U.S. Taxes," *Tax Foundation* (May 1, 2014) https://taxfoundation.org/it-takes-175-hours-us-business-comply-us-taxes
70   Williams, Walter E., "Who Pays What in Taxes?" *The New American* (Oct. 18, 2017) https://www.thenewamerican.com/reviews/opinion/item/27159-who-pays-what-in-taxes

Those at the highest income strata basically pay around 20% of their income in tax. [71] If even that much; the people in the top American income and wealth strata have often purchased enough latitude with national legislators that they can largely avoid taxation, or at worst, defer it in some manner so that they might effectively avoid it. This means that the brunt of taxation is generally borne by those in the income strata ranging between the 50.1 percentile and the 99.5 percentile, especially those above the 80th percentile. Maximum income tax rates top out, counting state and local jurisdiction taxation, somewhere in the high 40s for marginal income. Overall effective rates of taxation are much lower in effective terms, again, because of graduated and progressive rates.

The United States is hardly the only country that gives its rich, super rich, and oligarchs special tax privileges. American Exceptionalism in the taxation area, however, is not so much about what Americans *render to* Caesar in the form of what they pay in taxation. What is truly exceptional in the American context, at least in my view, is what a miserable package *Caesar renders back.* The United States provides some of the most miserable government benefits on Earth. Miserable, of course, unless you are a beneficiary of the military industrial complex, the higher-education industrial complex, agri-business, the health care industrial complex, or some other obese feline sucking at the government teat. American social spending by a broad measure is "somewhat below the OECD average," but this should not surprise you. We will discuss further economic, financial, and government spending aspects of American Exceptionalism in due course. Since we are talking about death and taxes, we toggle back to yet a further discussion of death in the American context. No discussion of death in the American context is complete without a discussion of death *by violence.* The occasional celebrity murder or not-so-occasional mass shooting event often lead the American media to start looking into the numbers on this.

---

71   "Tax Fairness Briefing Book," *Americans for Tax Fairness (2014)* (retrieved June 6, 2019) https://americansfortaxfairness.org/tax-fairness-briefing-booklet/fact-sheet-taxing-wealthy-americans/

The important number seems to be "2" as in "Second Amendment," the text of which suggests, in the collective mind of an insanely high number of Americans, "Thou Shalt Pack Heat Lest The Dark-Skinned People Get The Drop on You."

John Lennon of *The Beatles* was sufficiently iconic that we use his death in December 1980 as a measuring point. Some 35 years later by 2015, it was estimated that *1.15 million* Americans were *killed by guns* since he was shot near New York's Central Park; this works out to around 30,000 a year, which is more or less still the order of magnitude for American gun deaths. [72] By rate of gun deaths *per 100,000 people*, the United States comes in at 31st highest or so in the world, [73] but the other countries ahead of the US on the list are often in Latin America or the Caribbean, where gang violence is replete, or are war-torn places such as Iraq. In terms of prosperous industrial countries, levels of American gun violence are extraordinarily high. The rates of homicide from guns and other causes are several times higher than in Europe or in nearby Canada. Interestingly, to me, anyway, deaths by automobile accident are another area where Americans are world leaders. The United States finished first both per 100,000 and overall in that category among industrialized countries in a recent study. [74] The annual toll of 30,000 automobile accident deaths represents the same order of magnitude as American gun-related deaths. As Dmitry Orlov suggests (*see* footnote 22), one wonders whether Americans are rational enough to be permitted the private ownership of either firearms or automobiles. I assume you know that the answer is "of course not." For *seemingly preventable deaths*, drug overdose deaths [75] seem to blow away both gun deaths

72   Stuart, Tessa, "1.15 Million Americans Have Been Killed by Guns Since John Lennon's Death," *Rolling Stone* (Dec. 8, 2015) https://www.rollingstone.com/politics/politics-news/1-15-million-americans-have-been-killed-by-guns-since-john-lennons-death-43117/
73   Aizenman, Nurith, "Gun Violence: How the U.S. Compares With Other Countries," *NPR: Goats and Soda* (Oct. 6, 2017) https://www.npr.org/sections/goatsandsoda/2017/10/06/555861898/gun-violence-how-the-u-s-compares-to-other-countries
74   Leonard, Kimberly, "Why the U.S. Is a World Leader in Car Crash Deaths," *U.S. News & World Report* (July 6, 2016) https://www.usnews.com/news/articles/2016-07-06/the-us-is-a-world-leader-in-car-crash-deaths
75   Lopez, German, "America leads the world in drug overdose deaths —by a lot" *Vox.com* (June 28, 2017) https://www.vox.com/policy-and-politics/2017/6/28/15881246/drug-overdose-deaths-world

and automobile-related deaths. The United States, with around 5% of the world's population, has 27% of its drug overdose deaths! The magnitude of drug overdose deaths has recently been estimated in the range of 50,000 per year, of which 2/3 are opioid-related, and many of *those* drugs were prescribed by physicians. *Properly prescribed prescription drugs* are estimated to kill over 100,000 Americans per year, the same order of magnitude for annual deaths as stroke, which puts this category of deaths into fourth place on some lists of causes of death. If we include all categories of medical errors—whether malpractice by physicians or simply one of the countless possible professional mistakes—some studies estimate nearly *a quarter-million deaths per year* among Americans from medical error *alone*, making it the third leading cause of death in the US. [76]

Of the other leading causes of death in the United States, after the big two, heart disease and all forms of cancer, we have respiratory diseases, Alzheimer's disease, diabetes, influenza/pneumonia, kidney disease, suicide (including by firearms, drug overdose, and all other causes), septicemia, and liver diseases. The genius of American Exceptionalism is that Americans will categorically refuse to even recognize that nearly everything on this list is preventable or at least *manageable*. Through proper public health measures including proper medical staff training and individual choices to engage in an optimal diet, to take exercise and to make other healthier lifestyle decisions, most of the annual death totals associated with each of the causes of death on that list could be significantly reduced and life expectancy improved, accordingly. That, of course, is not how Americans roll.

Notwithstanding a seemingly large "nutraceutical" industry, health clubs and the like, there is actually surprisingly little overall American interest in healthy lifestyle or preventive health measures,

---

76   Sipherd, Ray, "The third-leading cause of death in US most doctors don't want you to know about," CNBC.com (Feb. 28. 2018) https://www.cnbc.com/2018/02/22/medical-errors-third-leading-cause-of-death-in-america.html

as opposed to magic pills, the costlier the better. I suspect that this is because Americans measure their expenditures on "health care" as *adding to* and *enhancing* the gross domestic product!

Thus, the United States proudly sports its vast health care industrial complex. Its many participants include professionals such as physicians, dentists, nurses and others, hospitals, nursing homes, "urgent care centers" and other health care facilities, "Big Pharma" (pharmaceutical manufacturers, distributors and retailers), and Big Finance (health insurers), among others. The United States proudly boasts the most costly "health care" in the world, closing in on 20% of GDP and exceeding $10,000 per person per year. [77] This expenditure level is around twice as much as that of the next highest-spending countries in the OECD. Despite the expensive health care system, the US sports the 12th highest obesity rate in the world, [78] although three of the countries ahead of the United States—Palau, Micronesia, and the Marshall Islands—are American military protectorates. According to the World Health Organization, the US sports the 37th best overall health care system; Canada comes in 30th; France comes in first. [79] In the recent American political environment, a number of politicians have been discussing "Medicare for All," a single, national health insurance payment system, currently available now only to the old and disabled. Studies from *right-wing* think tanks show that "Medicare for All" would likely save hundreds of billions or trillions of dollars and could even improve health care outcomes. [80] Needless to say, something that undermines the default American condition of ostensible *slavery* has little chance of getting through the multiple veto points endemic in the American political system.

---

77   Leonard, Kimberly, "Health spending passes $10,000 per person for first time," *Washington Examiner* (Dec. 6, 2017) https://www.washingtonexaminer.com/health-spending-passes-10-000-per-person-for-first-time
78   Dillinger, Jessica, "The Most Obese Countries in the World," *World Atlas* (last updated Feb. 16, 2018) https://www.worldatlas.com/articles/29-most-obese-countries-in-the-world.html
79   "World Health Organization's Ranking of the World's Health Systems," *The Patient Factor* (retrieved June 8, 2019) http://thepatientfactor.com/canadian-health-care-information/world-health-organizations-ranking-of-the-worlds-health-systems/
80   Baird, Addy, "Koch-backed study finds 'Medicare for All' would save U.S. trillions," *ThinkProgress* (July 30, 2018) https://thinkprogress.org/mercatis-medicare-for-all-study-0a8681353316/

Current levels of outrageously expensive inefficiency are quite profitable for all concerned, particularly for Big Pharma, which often raises drug prices dramatically every year, knowing that third-party insurers will likely pay for them, and for Big Finance, which has made "health insurance" wildly profitable. In the United States, where there is profit, there are political campaign contributions. It is hardly a coincidence that many of the most affluent American counties are in Greater Washington, D.C. [81] Lobbying for Big Pharma and Big Finance, and others who can afford lobbyists, is extremely lucrative as an "industry" in its own right. One would be well-advised to anticipate that this particular aspect of American Exceptionalism will not change in any meaningful way, at least before the rest of the American system collapses under the weight of its hefty moneyed special pleaders. Until death and taxes do us part.

---

[81]   "America's wealthiest counties: Six of top 10 richest counties in D.C. area," *WTOP.com* (Apr. 2, 2014) https://wtop.com/news/2014/04/americas-wealthiest-counties-six-of-top-10-richest-counties-in-dc-area/

8. THE NON-EMPIRE THAT DARE NOT SPEAK ITS IMPERIAL NAME

I T IS WIDELY UNDERSTOOD that the most complex political organizations ever assembled are empires. Empires surpass the "mere" nation-state by incorporating *multiple* nation states within their ambit. By the true measure of empire—imperial control of peripheral venues for the purpose of sucking them dry for the benefit of the core imperial power center—the American empire, despite being relatively young, not even a century old in its present form, is actually the largest and most successful of these imperial arrangements ever assembled. You are indeed astute, Dear Reader, as you have correctly observed that *empire* is simply the "macro" version of ostensible *slavery*. The "micro" version permeates virtually all aspects of life in the US, as you already know.

Nonetheless, the official doctrine, as taught to school children, is that *the United States is not an empire at all*. Americans are taught that empires involve colonies that issue postage stamps with the Queen's picture on them, whatever *postage stamps* are. Fortunately, *some people* in the American power structure are, even if only occasionally, willing to come clean on the "E word." [82]

---

82   A "senior adviser" to President George W. Bush, generally believed to be Karl Rove, is quoted by journalist Ron Suskind as follows: "We're an empire now, and when we act, we create our own reality. And while you're studying that reality—judiciously, as you will—we'll act again, creating other new realities, which you can study, too, and that's how things will sort out. We're history's actors . . . and you, all of you, will be left to just study what we do." Suskind, Ron, "Faith, Certainty and the Presidency of George W. Bush," *The New York Times* (Oct. 17, 2004) https://www.nytimes.com/2004/10/17/magazine/faith-certainty-and-the-presidency-of-george-w-bush.html

The American empire actually consists of two components, three counting the vast American homeland in North America.

The first and more obvious part of the empire consists of the official colonies: Puerto Rico, the Virgin Islands, American Samoa, Guam and the Northern Marianas, the semi-colonial enclave of the District of Columbia, and a few odd Pacific island military protectorates, *i.e.,* the Marshall Islands, Micronesia, and Palau, which, although technically independent nations, still have American postal zip codes. The United States picked up these colonies over the years, mostly during the Spanish-American War or during the world wars.

The second and less obvious, but far larger part of the empire consists of the less official peripheral colonies. Indeed, these colonies *appear* to be independent countries. Insofar as they are to greater or lesser extent *occupied by American troops,* whether on permanently "leased" bases, or "embedded" on the bases of the "host" nations, these are, nonetheless, colonial outposts of the American empire. These countries operate foreign policies and defense policies subservient to the United States, and, of course, economic policies favorable to the US, the imperial center. Amazingly, the colonies in this group actually include some of the largest and most powerful economies in the world, such as Germany, with over 40,000 American troops based there, Japan, with over 50,000 American troops based there, and Italy, with over 10,000 American troops based there. [83]

Before you snidely suggest, as I would, that this is what they get for losing World War II, we must also remember that the former colonial master of the United States, the United Kingdom, has over 8,000 American troops based on its territory; that is what it gets for *winning* World War II. South Korea also hosts over 30,000 American troops, and the American military also occupies some of the choicest real estate in that country. In one form or another,

---

[83] Merelli, Annalisa, "These are all the countries where the US has a military presence," *Quartz* (Apr. 2, 2015) https://qz.com/374138/these-are-all-the-countries-where-the-us-has-a-military-presence/

there are American troops on every continent, even on Antarctica, although American military personnel are officially there to do "scientific research." While the total and exact number of American troops stationed overseas is classified, it is believed that American troops are stationed in well over 100 countries [84] and perhaps substantially more than that. We note that there are around 200 or so countries on Earth, and thus more than half of them, and I suspect substantially more than that, have some American military presence within their territory.

Generally, for a country to avoid an American military presence on its soil, it must have nuclear weapons of its own. The United Kingdom is an exception; otherwise, it is safe to say that Russia, China, and North Korea are not part of the American empire, along with traditionally hostile countries such as Cuba and more recently hostile countries like Iran that have at least aligned themselves closely with non-American nuclear powers. India, Pakistan, and Israel, as nuclear powers, are American allies, but they have a measure of independence that most others without nuclear weapons do not. Interestingly, Britain and France, themselves nuclear powers and colonial imperial powers in their own right, are still mostly subservient to the far larger American empire.

In case you have not yet figured it out, the principal purpose of an empire is to impose favorable "trade" relationships on other countries. These favorable relationships usually involve decreeing low prices for the purchase of raw materials extracted from the colony, and then decreeing that the colony pays higher prices for goods and services sent back to the colony from the imperial center, an arrangement similar to prisoner commissary accounts. Thus, the British Empire turned one of the richest countries in the world, India, into one of the poorest countries in the world over the course of around 200 years of imperial squeezing. [85]

84   Turse, Nick, "Why Are US Special Operations Forces Deployed in Over 100 Countries?" *The Nation* (Jan. 7, 2014) https://www.thenation.com/article/why-are-us-special-operations-forces-deployed-over-100-countries/
85   Thiruvananthapuran, "British reduced India to one of the poorest countries: Shashi Tharoor," *Indian Express* (Dec. 21, 2016) https://indianexpress.com/article/india/british-reduced-india-to-one-of-the-poorest-countries-shashi-tharoor-4439070/

Of relevance to our discussion, the United States acquired what were ostensibly the rights to operate the then failing British Empire during World War II in a fire sale, perhaps more accurately a blitzkrieg sale. This deal enabled the United Kingdom to keep going long enough to survive the German onslaught and to allow Hitler to turn on his friends and let the Soviet Union end up doing the bulk of the bleeding for the Allied side. Historians refer to the secret meeting between FDR and Churchill as the birth of the Atlantic Charter, a cornerstone of the eventual NATO alliance. [86] In effect, however, this was a handover of the operation of the British Empire to what would become the American empire. To be sure, the United States had its own experience managing imperial possessions. For example, the US controlled the Philippines, which it would give up at the end of World War II with the proviso that it could maintain large military bases there for a *de facto* occupation. Still, the British Empire, thanks to its naval power, was really the first true global empire, on which, famously, "the sun never set." With much of the imperial capital of London reduced to rubble by the German onslaught, however, the *de facto* new owner and operator of the British Empire took it over in Washington by the end of the war. The head office of the new global empire was first manned by Harry Truman. Truman was a pleasant and folksy man who hailed from a corrupt urban Midwestern political machine. American political fixers anticipated that Truman would be much more malleable than the intellectual heavyweight and incumbent vice president Henry Wallace. Thus, they forced Wallace out as the candidate for vice president at the 1944 Democratic Convention. The first true American Emperor entered his role with a limited understanding of just what he was stepping into. Fortunately for all concerned within the American power establishment, Truman mostly did what he was told starting with unleashing the first and only atomic weapons ever used against human beings at Hiroshima and Nagasaki in Japan.

---

86   Klein, Christopher, "The Atlantic Charter's Surprising History," *History.com* (Oct. 28, 2018) https://www.history.com/news/the-atlantic-charters-surprising-history

The Soviet Union, which lost an inconceivable 20 million people, or one in seven of its citizens in the "Great Patriotic War," also emerged from the war as a major industrial power and with a fully mobilized military. While American atomic weapons kept the USSR from joining in the occupation of Japan, the Americans' development of the bomb strongly encouraged the USSR's efforts to get nuclear weapons of its own, a mission it accomplished within a few years of the end of the war.

Negotiations with Britain during the war permitted the American empire to expand from its existing realm, the Western hemisphere and a few Pacific islands, to a global one. This expansion ultimately involved managing the British Empire with its vast possessions in Africa and Asia and a "commonwealth" all over the globe. Negotiations involving Britain, France, and the Soviet Union after the war ended up dividing Europe between the American sphere of influence and military occupation in the west of Europe and the Soviet sphere of influence in the east. Some of this simply reflected the facts on the ground of where the Allied powers and their military forces happened to be. Thus, the hottest war ever, from 1939 to 1945, gave way to the so-called Cold War of 1945-1990. The imperial capitals of Washington and Moscow both benefited from their respective empires, as the occupying powers could impose "attitude adjustment" on their imperial vassals in the form of favorable economic conditions by which resources, including human resources, could be extracted on terms favorable to the imperial masters.

The Soviets did not establish true "market" prices, instead managing things for strategic and doctrinal reasons as much as for economic ones. For their part, the Americans very much established favorable market terms for American business. To be sure, the Americans were long doing this sort of thing in the Western hemisphere. By the 1950s and 1960s, the US could extend its reach virtually everywhere, outside of the Soviet or Chinese realms, of course.

If there was a fly in the ointment of American empire, it was that a largely air and naval-power-based empire was less stable at its periphery than the Soviet Union's more nearby land-based empire in Eastern Europe and other contiguous points, such as Mongolia and North Korea. Nonetheless, the American empire held on longer. As I write this in 2019, it is still holding on, however tenuously.

We return to our story. During the long Cold War, the American empire engaged in large-scale military operations in both Korea and Vietnam. These Asian ground wars both inflicted tremendous carnage on local populations. Tens of thousands of American troops were killed in action, plus hundreds of thousands of wounded. All of this occurred for seemingly little or no geopolitical advantage. Similar criticism could be leveled at the post-Cold War American military adventures in Central and Western Asia, notably Iraq and Afghanistan. These, of course, were originally started to fight "terrorism" in the aftermath of the September 11th events. Those post-Cold War wars, in turn, left thousands of Americans dead, tens of thousands wounded, and untold numbers of locals killed and wounded. Similarly, both of those nations and neighboring ones (such as Syria) have been entirely destabilized, for seemingly little or no geopolitical advantage. Are you sensing a pattern? I give you this brief history, featuring incredible futility at incredible human and financial cost because it has been the hallmark of American behavior since the United States became a global empire in the 1940s. [87] Why exactly the United States continues to engage in these costly and bloody ground wars in Asia is not understood by most Americans. The "why" is actually quite simple, but only if it were permissible for Americans to recognize that their nation *is actually an empire*. And presently, it is an empire nearing the end of its rope. Even the long-favorable terms by which it has been operating against the rest of the world can no longer provide the measure of economic benefit they

---

87   The US spends more on "defense" than the next seven nations, combined. "U.S. Defense Spending Compared to Other Countries," *Peter G. Peterson Foundation* (May 3, 2019) https://www. pgpf.org/chart-archive/0053_defense-comparison

once did. The American working class, whose members once lived solidly middle-class lifestyles, was kicked to the proverbial curb. Even the vaunted middle class of technocrats and managers finds itself ever more vulnerable; only the people of "the 1%," and really only *half of them*, have any real stake or advantage remaining in the rapidly contracting American imperial system. Because *they* benefit, however, the system goes on, and seemingly cannot be modified for anyone else's benefit.

None of this is new. Writing in the 1930s, *before* FDR's turnkey acquisition of the British Empire franchise made the United States a truly global empire, General Smedley Butler, the most decorated member of the United States Marine Corps of that time, discussed the practical function of the American military in terms no one has ever equaled [88] :

I spent 33 years and four months in active military service and during that period I spent most of my time as a high class muscle man for Big Business, for Wall Street and the bankers. In short, I was a racketeer, a gangster for capitalism. I helped make Mexico and especially Tampico safe for American oil interests in 1914. I helped make Haiti and Cuba a decent place for the National City Bank boys to collect revenues in. I helped in the raping of half a dozen Central American republics for the benefit of Wall Street. I helped purify Nicaragua for the International Banking House of Brown Brothers in 1902-1912. I brought light to the Dominican Republic for the American sugar interests in 1916. I helped make Honduras right for the American fruit companies in 1903. In China in 1927 I helped see to it that Standard Oil went on its way unmolested. Looking back on it, I might have given Al Capone a few hints. The best he could do was to operate his racket in three districts. I operated on three continents.

American school children, even those who venture into advanced degrees in political science, are taught that the United States is "the

---

[88]   Butler, Smedley D., *War is a Racket,* Round Table Press (1935).

world's policeman" because we are a benign and wonderful people and do so as a service to humanity; most people think of "American Exceptionalism" as somehow related to this. To the less naïve, we tell them that the global international order, including institutions like the United Nations and the World Trade Organization, or regional alliances like NATO, are propped up by the Americans because the present international order of global stability is good for American business interests. Furthermore, the global order is good for our trading partners, and this is good for the American people and American businesses. We are all about "growth." This is, of course, much closer to what is actually happening. This is all good as far as it goes. It still fails, however, to explain the *scale* of American military presence—seemingly global, and seemingly everywhere.

More importantly, it fails to explain the somewhat unusual history of the mightiest military force in the world. Other than occasionally kicking around pint-sized nations such as Grenada or Panama, this mighty military, even when backed by vast vassal "coalitions of the willing," seems unable to win decisive military victories let alone "win the peace" virtually anywhere, be it in Korea, or in Vietnam, or in the Persian Gulf, or even in defeated Iraq, Afghanistan, Somalia, or Libya. The American military is probably second to none these days in getting people killed including, of course, its own. But whatever "policy objectives" a "strong military" is supposed to achieve continue to remain elusive, at best.

The explanation for this apparent enigma is shockingly simple, if one dispenses with the official nonsense about the United States being a "shining beacon" or "city on the hill" or more laughably, a "force for good." The United States is none of those things: it is, simply, an empire. It is the largest empire in the history of human civilization in terms of both its geography and the population it effectively controls. Virtually every country on Earth is part of the imperium, with the critical exceptions of actual imperial rivals and their own vassal states, notably China, Russia, and their respective satellites, and a few odd outliers like Cuba, Venezuela, North Korea, Iran, Syria, Lebanon, and interestingly, Israel.

With the exception of its own official vassal colonies and captive "countries" in the Pacific, which, as we have noted, even sport American postal zip codes, the rest of the planet is not *formally* under American sovereign control. Only the truly ignorant, however, which, sadly, includes most Americans, believe that the only possible configuration of an empire is the formal one. The informal but *de facto* empire is still very much an empire. In the case of the American one, the US maintains an almost universal military presence *to enforce its will*, specifically its foreign and economic policies. It will enforce whatever additional policies it needs to in the interests of maintaining the empire. Once one understands the life cycles of empires, to wit, that like any living organism, they are born, age, strengthen, and then weaken, and eventually die, then one can quickly understand why the American empire with its mighty military has been largely spinning its wheels for at least 75 years.

We must first observe that the very existence of the United States as an entity independent of European empire is *itself* a study in imperial dynamics. Thus, we first examine the nascent American republic. It was hardly coincidental that the spanking new US sent its two greatest polymaths Benjamin Franklin and Thomas Jefferson as its early envoys *to France*—the leading, rival global empire of Britain. From that perspective, Franklin and Jefferson could provide their foundling government with an understanding of imperial dynamics that the American republic could use to play the more powerful Europeans off against each other. By doing so, the US achieved not only independence, but eventually achieved imperial status of its own. Similarly, it was hardly coincidental when the American empire essentially doubled in size overnight at the check-writing hand of Thomas Jefferson himself, when, without hesitation, he acquired the Louisiana Purchase from then war-weary and flailing France. This was a similar mechanism to how FDR later acquired operational control of the British Empire, which we will discuss shortly.

The vibrant young American empire found that it could easily expand against the weaker Spanish Empire when it acquired

Florida, and later, when it expanded against independent Mexico in acquiring what is now Texas and much of the American West.

In its first century of its operation, the American empire was so strong that it even had the luxury of surviving an internal revolution. When the agrarian slave-based economy of the American South rebelled against the broader industrial (wage) slave-based economy of the North in the 1860s in an economic struggle over methods of production (*i.e.,* slavery) and terms of trade (tariff issues), the American empire actually *strengthened* and even added Alaska in an acquisition from the Russians called "Seward's Folly." The American Civil War proved to be the world's first all-out modern, industrial-based conflict. In terms of deaths, that four-year conflict inflicted more casualties upon Americans than any single other conflict, significant for an empire that has been at war of some kind for nearly all of its existence. Indeed, Civil War casualties were in the order of magnitude of all other American military conflicts *combined.* [89]

The industrialists of the North ultimately prevailed, of course. After that war, now duly organized as a modern industrial state, the United States solidified its contiguous, continental internal empire. It added transcontinental telegraph and railroad services, and beefed up its military presence throughout its own territory.

By the end of the 19th century, having already acquired Alaska and having picked off the independent kingdom of Hawaii in a commercial coup, the confident "middle" stage American empire could now pick off the weakest remaining European power with holdings nearby. This, of course, was Spain. The Spanish-American War handed the United States control of Cuba and the Philippines, Guam, and Puerto Rico, the latter two still American colonies to this day.

The 20th century began with the Americans having their own continent largely secure in a contiguous land empire, with Alaska relatively easy to reach by water, as well as an effective trans-Pacific

---

89   "American War Deaths Throughout History," *Military Factory* (retrieved June 14, 2019) https://www.militaryfactory.com/american_war_deaths.asp

empire. The United States had exercised economic and military dominance over a less-formal empire in Latin America since the early part of the 19th century. The 20th century has been called "the American century," although it could also rightly be called "the age when genocide met industrialization and got *really* effective." [90]

As a matter of world history, with the exception of the American Civil War, the wars fought between 1815 and 1914 were comparatively limited at least, by world standards of brutality, perhaps because those wars did not require the full participation of all of Europe's major powers at any one time. In the quarter century after 1914, however, all of this would change spectacularly.

Although the spark that led to the First World War consisted of what appeared to be the random assassination of an Austrian archduke in a backwater part of the Balkans, the harsher reality was that the forces of industrialization and the concentration of industrial and financial capital were at work in the great European capitals. The great empires of Europe, the British, French, German, Austro-Hungarian, Russian, and the Ottoman (Turkish), quickly paired off against each other. They discovered how quickly each could unleash their respective military-industrial complexes on their opponents. The Great War of 1914-1918 still saw significant troop movement on horseback particularly from the Turkish and Russian sides. That war also introduced the airplane into combat, mostly for reconnaissance and intelligence rather than dropping bombs as would be the case in later wars, although of course there was also significant air-to-air combat. Firearms such as machine guns and other munitions and the ability to deliver them more accurately had advanced dramatically in the previous hundred years. Chemical weapons were deployed in

---

90   The career of German Fritz Haber is remarkably evocative of both the advances and horrors of the 20th century. Haber gave the world the Haber-Bosch process for manufacturing nitrogen fertilizer (mostly from fossil fuel) that is the indispensable component of "the green revolution" that ultimately increased agrarian productivity and in turn enabled the world's population to explode from barely a billion-and-a-half people at the beginning of the 20th century, to over seven billion by the end of it. Haber, a German Jew, was also instrumental in the German weapons program that led to the horrific poison gases used in World War I, and the precursors of the very chemicals that the German state would use to industrially slaughter the Jewish people during World War II. *See* "Fritz Haber," *Science History Institute* (Dec. 7, 2017) https://www.sciencehistory.org/historical-profile/fritz-haber

significant magnitude for the first and last time (at least legally) in a war of this scale.

The United States eventually intervened in the First World War after it had raged for three years, intervening on the British and French side. The Russians were about to drop out, having their own internal problems which would eventually result in the Russian Revolution and over 70 years of the Union of Soviet Socialist Republics. By bringing its own industrial might, as well as a large number of fresh troops, American intervention almost certainly ensured that the British and French side prevailed.

Now, over a century after the close of the Great War, there is still disagreement as to its causes. I would suggest that it is appropriate to look at the life cycles of the various empires involved in it. Then the causes of the Great War become more apparent, as well as providing a cautionary tale for the present state of the American empire.

By 1914, the American empire was actually at the height of its industrial power. It was still importing millions of workers for its industrial enterprises, mostly from Eastern and Southern Europe by this time. The "progressive movement" had sparked a number of "reforms," such as graduated income taxation and a central bank. The American empire had consolidated its control of the entirety of Central North America from sea to shining sea, as well as Alaska, Hawaii, and the offshore goodies it picked up from Spain. Its imperial exploitation of the rest of the Western hemisphere was operating at full bore. The Americans looked across the Atlantic to the Old World, and saw that the great European empires were at each other's throats. The rising German empire joined the longer-established Austro-Hungarian Empire and the overextended and terminally ill Turkish/Ottoman Empire in battling the late stage British and French empires and the terminally ill Russian Empire. For its part, the US sat thousands of miles away, and its economy actually profited handsomely from the war. [91]

91   See Frum, David, "The Real Story of How America Became an Economic Superpower," *The Atlantic* (Dec. 24, 2014) https://www.theatlantic.com/international/archive/2014/12/the-real-story-of-how-america-became-an-economic-superpower/384034/

As the withdrawal of Russia (what would become the Russian Revolution was raging internally) could have tipped the balance in favor of the German side, the British eventually persuaded their American counterparts to enter the war on the British side. With the mighty American empire involved, the war was soon won by the Allied powers. Being on the winning side in the aftermath of the Great War, the US was set to take a grander role on the world stage. American schoolchildren learn that "the isolationists" intervened and kept the United States from joining the League of Nations, and otherwise from suppressing British and French demands for war reparations from the defeated German side which were, in fact, *largely recycled back to the United States to repay British and French war debts to the Americans.* By the conclusion of the Great War, the American empire was actually still consolidating its own hold on Western hemisphere and its own Pacific possessions, and the American industrial base had finally fully "staffed up" to the point where the US no longer needed vast numbers of new immigrants to achieve peak output.

Simply put, the prevailing American policymakers of the time concluded that the United States did not need to inject itself into a larger role in European affairs other than to try to derail the Bolsheviks in Russia and to collect war debts, of course. A larger role in world affairs was deemed not consistent with American interests of a Western Hemisphere and Pacific-based empire. Indeed, by the 1920s, immigration was curtailed dramatically, and financial speculation exploded. "The Roaring Twenties" were on. The Roaring Twenties, of course, culminated in the stock market crash of October 1929, followed by the Great Depression.

In the same period, the United States had demobilized its military following the Great War, and reduced the man-power size of its military forces in the 1930s, just as the Japanese were establishing the Greater East Asian Co-Prosperity Sphere and bombing targets in China. Germany was also establishing its own European empire with the Anschluss, and Italy was militarizing its own colonies in

Africa. For its part, the US was still flexing its military muscle in Latin America, but mostly staying out of the "Old World." And in the 1930s, of course, the Great Depression resulted in a collapse of both global and domestic demand for American products, massive collapses in asset values and, of course, massive unemployment and attendant loss of income. While much of the world suffered through the Great Depression, many countries had various levels of social services to alleviate the suffering. For its part, the non-capitalist Soviet Union was rapidly industrializing, and suffered less economically as a result of the Depression than much of Europe. Of course, it was starting from a lower level of prosperity, and its totalitarian leader, Josef Stalin, ruthlessly sent countless Soviet citizens to gulags or firing squads. Germany, of course, had the economic trauma of the Weimar Republic, and eventually installed the National Socialist regime of Adolf Hitler and ramped up for war. Meanwhile, back in the United States, President Herbert Hoover, an avowed capitalist, engaged in classic sado-monetarist policies such as higher tariffs, lower national spending, and serious contractions of the money supply. As technical matters, these are excellent ways to kick an economy when it is already down. Being a Republican, the more right-wing of the two right-wing political parties in the official American political duopoly, Hoover was just not doctrinally equipped to deal with that scale of human suffering other than, of course, to cause more of it.

Meanwhile, in America's then most populous and most important state, New York, a young patrician governor named Franklin D. Roosevelt was working on implementing many of the progressive and pro-human policies that his innovative working-class predecessor, Alfred E. Smith, had put in place, with some success. After winning the 1932 presidential election, FDR would bring Smith's ideas and some of Smith's people, but not Smith himself, to Washington, and "the New Deal" was on. The New Deal set up national pensions for old people, increased rights of workers, such as a minimum wage and a workers' compensation scheme for injuries, and large-scale government work programs to alleviate poverty, among many other measures. These were all dramatic developments in the American context, though modest compared to many European social welfare programs. All of FDR's New Deal programs were inconsistent with basic American doctrine (ostensible slavery) and have been fought by American politicians, including many "Democrats," since FDR implemented them.

One area of "economic stimulus" that was starting to rev up the American economy by the end of the 1930s was selling war materiel to the Allied powers (mostly Britain), and of course, re-stocking American armories. Ultimately, the industrial ramp-up caused by what would become the Second World War is widely credited with taking the United States out of the Great Depression and into its unrivaled post-war prosperity.

Shortly before American entry into that war, FDR saw opportunity. In the same manner in which Jefferson waited for French emperor Napoleon to weaken to the point where he would offer some gem to the Americans for an extreme bargain price which materialized in the 1803 Louisiana Purchase that provided the United States with something like one-third of what is now the continental United States, FDR bided his time. For its part, Europe proceeded to tear itself apart in the Second World War. The American empire had reached a different place twenty years after it refused to join the League of Nations at Versailles. The United States had more or less fully absorbed its immigrant waves of industrial cannon fodder and cut off most immigration in the 1920s as a consequence. In fact, the Americans had built out the greatest industrial capacity that the world had ever seen, albeit largely unused because of the ongoing Depression, and was in the perfect position to exploit a global empire opportunity.

That opportunity presented itself in the early 1940s as Mr. Churchill met Mr. Roosevelt on *The Prince of Wales* off the coast of Newfoundland, and made the deal-of-the-American-century. Britain got what it needed to avoid being overrun by the Nazis via the "Lend Lease" program, as it handed the United States effective operational control of its global empire at a moment it was not really in a position to manage it anyway. [92]

Like the French in 1803, the British were fully engaged in a major war and could barely hold on to most of their empire as it was. The right to operate the British Empire on American terms was, of course, a staggering addition, as that empire literally included elements on every continent. Canadian Newfoundland was still a British colony during the Second World War, as were many Caribbean islands and British Honduras in North America and British Guyana in South America. Huge swaths of Africa and Asia were part of the British Empire. Malta, Cyprus, and Gibraltar in Europe were part of the empire. Britain notionally remained "sovereign" after the deal, and notionally remained the imperial ruler. Ultimately, however, the operational economic benefit of the empire, as most clearly demonstrated by the opportunity to maintain American military bases in these places or in some cases, British bases effectively under American control, and the ability to exert "attitude adjustment" on anyone not playing ball with the new American empire, was firmly established.

Of course, the United States already maintained its own sphere of influence in the Western Hemisphere pretty much this way for the better part of the prior hundred years. By the end of the Second World War, the United States could add most of Central and Western Europe to the equation, as well as much of Africa, the Middle East, Central and Southeast Asia, and even Japan. This dispensation not only held for decades of unbridled American prosperity, but the American empire actually expanded to include most of *Eastern Europe* during

---

92   The secret meeting, as you would expect, of course, has been reported in substantially more anodyne terms than the *de facto* surrender of the British Empire to the Americans in exchange for cash and other war assistance that I assert took place. For example, the State Department's historian reports that, "Both countries agreed not to seek territorial expansion; to seek the liberalization of international trade; to establish freedom of the seas, and international labor, economic, and welfare standards. Most importantly, both the United States and Great Britain were committed to supporting the restoration of self-governments for all countries that had been occupied during the war and allowing all peoples to choose their own form of government." Eschner, Kat, "Months Before Pearl Harbor, Churchill and Roosevelt Held a Secret Meeting of Alliance," *Smithsonian* (Aug. 14, 2017) https://www.smithsonianmag.com/smart-news/months-pearl-harbor-churchill-and-roosevelt-secret-meeting-180964435/

the 1990s after the implosion of the Soviet Union. [93]

The industrial position of the United States was perfectly aligned with its imperial position for at least the first 25 years after the Second World War, what I would call "the American Quarter Century." Not only was the US the world's premier industrial economy, but its principal industrial rivals, Japan, Germany, Britain, and France, were in ruins. The Americans' principal military rival, the Soviet Union, had just suffered calamitously in the war it "won," with over one in seven of its citizens killed during what it called the Great Patriotic War, including millions of Jews murdered in the Nazi Holocaust.

And so, with both international markets to sell into, and a new empire to buy raw materials from on favorable terms, coupled with a huge pent-up domestic demand after a long Depression and War, the mighty American industrial machine ramped up to produce consumer goods. Together with the American advertising and propaganda machine, American industry reached output never before achieved. For decades, working-class people literally found themselves elevated to the lifestyles of middle and upper-middle-class people in what appeared to be an inter-generationally sustainable way.

This period was also the heyday of American oil production, which was so prolific that the United States could literally impose price controls on retail gasoline. Indeed, the capitalistic American state also imposed price controls on air travel and telecommunications and many other areas of the economy. Even though some Americans might look back on that era fondly, official doctrine is that price controls of that kind are the indicia of *socialist backwaters*. This is understandable, as Americans invariably learn to forget any knowledge that does not support the current whims of those in power, particularly those with economic power. During

---

93   The imperial lesson endeth there, as, for the first time in its imperial history, the American empire finally overreached, and now can no longer maintain itself. Like the cartoon character Wile E. Coyote, the American empire stepped off a cliff, but has not quite fallen to a crash yet. More on that later.

this same period, the American military was called into two large-scale imperial adventures and quite a few smaller ones. The question that American children are taught to ask concerning the Korean and Vietnam conflicts is why the powerful American war machine could not achieve a decisive victory over seemingly weaker forces, and in Korea could not do so with a supposed mandate of the United Nations. As a historical matter, China was then represented by the Nationalist exiles on Taiwan, rather than by the government of the actual country of China. The Soviet Union, in a procedural miscalculation, boycotted the United Nations Security Council in protest of actions against its friend China, and thereby allowed the American empire official cover and license to operate without the check on its power of a United Nations Security Council veto. [94]

We will return to that question shortly. First, we must examine why, in more recent years, an even larger American empire, now including "coalitions of the willing" that even included former Warsaw Pact members in Eastern Europe, proved incapable of achieving decisive victory over a war-weary, sanctions-damaged Iraq, or for that matter, over irregulars and warlords in Afghanistan and later in Iraq. I suggest that this is easier to understand than the Vietnam and Korean conflicts, because by the time of the first and second Gulf Wars and the Afghan campaign, the American empire had finally reached the "spent" point, having expanded well beyond the point that the empire was even providing a positive return to the enterprise.

Furthermore, largely because its political power apparatus was captured by financial technocrats rather than by industrialists, the United States had made a number of fateful, self-defeating decisions. One of the most important and devastating of these decisions was permitting Communist China to enter the World Trade Organization, and then, outsourcing a lion's share of American industrial production *to China*. These actions violated two cardinal rules of running a decent empire: (1) never give up *real* high-value

---

94   "Soviets boycott United Nations Security Council," *History.com* (Feb. 22, 2019) https://www.history.com/this-day-in-history/soviets-boycott-united-nations-security-council

productive functions to anyone else, and (2) never, ever place reliance for strategic goodies, especially manufactured ones, on a country that is *not in the empire*. The significance of these mistakes cannot be overstated. China cannot be disciplined the same way that ordinary imperial vassals can be, *i.e.,* by the "attitude adjustment" of having American troops based in the country, or by other American levers of power. The US has attempted a menacing encirclement of China, including maintenance of large numbers of troops in South Korea and Japan, Guam, and lately, Australia. For good measure, American troops in Afghanistan are not far away from China either. The longstanding and close alliance between the United States and Taiwan has also proven inadequate to the task of managing China as an "associate" of the empire. China maintains the world's largest standing army in man-power, a nuclear arsenal and the ability to deliver it anywhere, and because of the decisions that made American financiers rich at the expense of everyone else, China holds trillions of dollars in American debt instruments that it could dump if push came to shove. Thus, unlike American vassal states, China can push back on the American Imperium in the way that it values its own currency, in the way that it deals with technology transfers, *i.e.,* favorably to itself, and in numerous other ways, such as trade practices about which the Americans often cry foul. Of course, the US simply cannot dictate the terms of its relationship with China quite as forcefully as it does to most of the world, including Europe, whose European Union mechanism often appears to act contrary to American interests, but in a much more limited manner than one would think.

In short, like the very late-stage Roman Empire or, for that matter, the late-stage British Empire, the logistics of maintaining the vast, global American empire are staggering. Maintaining that empire no longer appears viable, although the American military machine can effectively inflict violence against almost anyone almost anywhere. As of the 21st century, the American military generally can no longer really achieve *anything* of meaningful strategic value.

Returning to our story, you will rightly point out that both the Korean and Vietnam adventures took place at moments when the American industrial machine and overall American power was at its peak strength. Indeed, the US at the time of the conflicts in Korea and Vietnam was the post-World War II behemoth that supplied much of the world's industrial output at a time its main rivals were still licking their wounds from the Second World War. So, you might ask, what happened?

Both adventures featured tactical and strategic failures, and both involved a monumental failure of imagination. One such failure of imagination produced "the domino theory" which suggested that somehow permitting the self-determination of the people of the world would result in those people wanting to join the American empire. [95] Any deviation from this disposition could only be the result of something insidious, such as international communism.

Further, both Korea and Vietnam each had their own specifically local dimensions. We are linking them together here to ascertain why the American empire did not achieve its strategic goals in both places, to wit, absorbing *the entirety* of both Korea and Vietnam into the American empire, in the same manner that the US more successfully absorbed Japan, Western Europe, and Latin America before them.

The Korean adventure began in the late 1940s when the Chinese-backed North invaded the American-backed South, pushing Southern forces to the Southern tip of the Korean peninsula at Pusan. Still fresh from World War II, American forces, led by the brilliant and egomaniacal general Douglas MacArthur, reinvaded the Korean peninsula. The Americans pushed the Northern-invading forces back up to the northern part of the Korean peninsula. The problem with doing this was not tactical; tactics employed during the Korean conflict were brilliant in many ways.

The problem was actually strategic imperial hubris. As in the

95   Llewellyn, J., et al, "The Domino Theory," *Alpha History* (accessed June 6, 2019) https://alphahistory.com/coldwar/domino-theory/

American Revolution, where American insurgents had the ace-in-the-hole of a superpower ally in France, North Korean insurgents had an ace-in-the-hole ally in China. The newly established People's Republic of China was also called "Red China" to recognize the communist school colors, and to distinguish it from "Nationalist China," whose leadership had by then fled to Taiwan. Red China was on good terms with the coming superpower to its North, the Soviet Union. Because the Americans had just acquired a vast global empire from the British, it did not dawn on American policymakers to consider both the limits of their own imperial power, or the interests of other would-be superpowers. Simply put, the Americans successfully deluded themselves about China, *i.e.*, they seemed to genuinely believe that the exiled *Kuo Min Tang* government of Chiang Kai-shek sitting across the Taiwan Straits on the island of Formosa was, in fact, the actual government of China, one of the world's two largest countries by population. It was as if the Americans believed that the actual rulers of China, Mao Tse-tung and the communists, despite their control of the Chinese mainland and millions of mobilized, if under-equipped troops were only a temporary annoyance, and as a result, they seriously underestimated Red China's commitment to its allies. Unfortunately, a committed standing army numbering in the millions is usually hard to ignore, no matter how strong your belief that it is not really a factor.

Thus, the American push of Kim Il Sung's North Korean forces toward the Yalu River and China resulted, inevitably, in waking up the not-so-sleepy giant of Communist China. Together with support from the nearby Soviet Union, the North Koreans were more than up to the task of holding the American military at bay, and ultimately, after untold thousands of casualties on all sides, a stalemate ensued. An unpleasant truce has resulted in a conflict that legally and technically still rages on almost seven decades later, with some peculiar ongoing annoyances. The notoriously paranoid and insular North Korean regime has even managed to acquire nuclear weapons and regularly tests those missiles to deliver them somewhere. As a historical matter, the steadiest hand for the United States during the post-war period was also its most successful military man, General Dwight Eisenhower. "Ike," it should be noted, even after his presidency, often referred to himself as "General Eisenhower" rather than "President Eisenhower." Ike rather quickly saw that the Korean adventure was going nowhere, and used his considerable *gravitas* to engineer the ultimately uncomfortable, but lasting, truce. Also during his term, he calmly endured the year 1956, in which the American colonies of Britain and France joined American-not-quite-colony Israel in causing the Suez Crisis, an invasion of Egypt to establish European control of an Egyptian waterway and to remove irritant Egyptian President Nasser. Both the Soviet Union and Eisenhower pressured these American colonies (and Israel) to back off, and they ultimately did. Britain was particularly humiliated by whole affair. Some believed that this emboldened the Soviet Union to invade Hungary, which it did almost immediately after the Suez crisis. This led to a rather poignant water polo match between the USSR and Hungary at the Sydney Summer Olympics, which were held in November that year because of the austral summer. And once again, Eisenhower calmly managed to avoid getting the planet blown up, recognizing that the Soviet Union would be permitted greater freedom of action within its own sphere of influence, which, after all, he himself had been instrumental in establishing in the immediate aftermath of the Second World War. Perhaps, unfortunately, from the standpoint of imperial governance, Eisenhower's sideman, Vice President Richard Nixon, lost a very close election in 1960 to John F. Kennedy.

Unfortunately, steady-hand Eisenhower also employed the Flying Dulles Brothers, particularly the early CIA man and world-class maniac Alan Dulles. The Dulles brothers were not so good at imperial management. They were, however, utterly brilliant at the sort of dirty tricks that involved parachuting American spies deep into Soviet territory where they were invariably captured, and after an unpleasant interrogation, shot. The Dulles brothers had prepared a welcome surprise for the new Democratic President, a mission to unseat the inconvenient Soviet ally, Fidel Castro in Cuba, by landing Cuban expats on the beach at the Cuban water body of *Bahia de Cochinos* (Bay of Pigs). [96]

This would prove to go about as well as many of the Dulles brothers' other dirty tricks operations. That is to say, badly. It is not clear as a historical matter if the Bay of Pigs led directly to the Cuban Missile Crisis the following year (1962), but it is a very good bet. The brinksmanship of possible nuclear war was certainly dangerous, but less dangerous than historically suggested, as the Americans quietly withdrew some missiles from the Soviet Union's doorstep in Turkey in exchange for the Soviets pulling their missiles out of Cuba. Of particular interest is that Cuba is the fourth closest country to the United States proper. Obviously, the US has land borders with Canada and Mexico, and two Bering Strait islands are very close to Russia, then the USSR, followed by Cuba; maybe the Bahamas are closer, but what do I know? Cuba itself had even once been an actual American protectorate! Indeed, Cuba was forced to give the United States a permanently "leased" military base at Guantanamo Bay, another example of American Exceptionalism we will discuss later, which the US maintains to this very day. The former American colony joining the rival Soviet empire was more than a little galling.

Of course, the American "intelligence" establishment was not at all pleased with Kennedy's handling of the Bay of Pigs affair by trying to go in lightly and stealthily without American air power in order to maintain deniability.

On another continent, Asia, it was not clear what the "intelligence" services told Kennedy that required sending "military advisers" to try to bail out the former French colony in Vietnam against incursions from its northern Communist neighbor. [97] An all-out Communist invasion of the American colony South Vietnam did not seem that far-fetched. South Vietnam enjoyed an unpleasant

---

96   History.com staff, "The Bay of Pigs invasion begins," *History.com* (Apr. 16, 2019) https://www.history.com/this-day-in-history/the-bay-of-pigs-invasion-begins
97   It is also not clear what involvement "intelligence services" had in Kennedy's unfortunate assassination a year later in 1963, after "military advisers" were in place in Vietnam.

and corrupt dictatorship allied with the United States, a consistent pattern for the American empire. The American empire often operates best when allying with unpleasant dictators who take their orders from Washington. In any event, the ultimate decision to escalate hostilities in Vietnam to prevent the fall of an American colony like a domino was probably not a heavy lift. After Kennedy's assassination in 1963, the management of the American empire fell to the Vice President, a petulant former senator from Texas named Lyndon Baines Johnson (LBJ). LBJ shepherded a number of Kennedy programs to fruition and added quite a few of his own, including most famously the Civil Rights Act, the Voting Rights Act, and the Great Society social welfare programs including medical assistance for the poor, or "Medicaid," and medical care for the elderly and disabled, "Medicare." These programs, like the New Deal, were contrary to basic American doctrine (*ostensible slavery*) and hence, they have been under assault ever since. LBJ suggested that expanding civil rights to people of color would cost the Democratic Party the South for a generation. It has proven longer. LBJ's *real* offense, of course, like FDR's before him, was *trying to ameliorate the cruelties of capitalism.*

Unfortunately, LBJ's other great legacy was the ramping up of American forces in Vietnam. As the 1964 election approached, an election that LBJ would win in a landslide over Republican ideologue Barry Goldwater, things were heating up in Southeast Asia. To this day, there is still uncertainty as to whether LBJ actually staged the Gulf of Tonkin Affair or whether he was played into pretending it was important and used it as an excuse to ramp up American involvement in Vietnam. [98] By the time that the Vietnam conflict ended with the embarrassing images of personnel being evacuated by helicopter from an embassy roof, over 58,000 Americans were killed in the conflict and hundreds of thousands were wounded, together with an unknown and incredibly large number of Vietnamese, Cambodians, and Laotians killed or wounded.

---

98   Greenspan, Jesse, "The Gulf of Tonkin Incident 50 Years Ago," *History.com* (Aug. 31, 2018) https://www.history.com/news/the-gulf-of-tonkin-incident-50-years-ago

Of relevance to our broader discussion of the American empire is the question of why the United States found itself pouring in vast quantities of blood and treasure into what was once a lush tropical paradise. We must ask where the United States was in the imperial life cycle. The sad reality is that the US was farther along its own imperial life timeline than one would have thought. Although the American global empire was barely twenty years old, its trans-Pacific Empire was nearing seventy. Its Western hemispheric domination, however, was nearly a century-and-a-half old. The original imperial marching orders arose in 1823 with the Monroe Doctrine. [99]

Nonetheless, because of the speed with which these developments occurred, the United States hit mature status as an empire almost immediately upon absorbing its global acquisitions. Much of this was because the British Empire that the United States was assuming and evidently, the parts of the French empire that the Americans also undertook to manage, were far older, and long past their own sell-by dates.

Still, besides the place of the United States in the imperial life cycle, there were other familiar features concerning the Vietnam adventure. As in Korea, American policymakers overestimated their own mightiness, particularly when measured against the relative might of the Red Chinese who, after nearly 20 years of American discounting, still had not gone anywhere, even as Chiang Kai-shek and his exiles in Taiwan still held China's U.N. Security Council seat and veto. Of course, the Americans also underestimated the commitment, as well as the strength, of the Soviet Union. Most disturbingly, US policymakers did not understand the commitment of the Vietnamese themselves, who proved to be extraordinarily dedicated adversaries. The North Vietnamese and their Viet Cong allies dug in, literally, as they fought to protect their homeland from foreign interlopers. Somehow, it never quite dawned on American policymakers let alone most of the American public that much of

99   "Monroe Doctrine," *Office of the Historian, Department of State* (retrieved June 16, 2019) https://history.state.gov/milestones/1801-1829/monroe

the world would perceive the Americans as *foreign interlopers and invaders*. This blind spot remains in place to this day. As usual, the Americans also underestimated the vast unpopularity of their own corrupt vassals in the South Vietnamese government. Finally, the US, so used to extracting the benefits of being an empire from its global imperial vassal states and colonies, utterly failed to account for the costs of the intervention.

Financially, these costs were so extreme that they ultimately resulted in large transfers of gold out of the United States to pay for the war. By 1971, President Richard Nixon had to stop gold outlays altogether and literally changed the world's organizing financial arrangement to a pure fiat currency scheme, finally ending the international gold standard. [100] Militarily, it is widely believed that the "quagmire" supposedly sapped the Americans' fighting ability so much that the "lessons of Vietnam," whatever they are, still remain relevant in some way. [101] Socially, Vietnam also imposed significant costs to the American empire. Anti-draft and anti-war protests and attendant social unrest would prove to be some of the most severe since the Civil War draft protests 100 years earlier. [102] Of course, inflicting the carnage of the Vietnam War on a far-off people for no apparent strategic advantage presented enormous moral costs, as well. All of these costs, in turn, undermined the simultaneous social transformations that President Lyndon Johnson was attempting domestically with the Civil Rights and Great Society programs. Of course, empires often believe that they can do everything at once. Because of course, they are empires. There are limits to being a global empire, however, particularly when such an empire bumps

---

100   Ghizoni, Sandra Kollen, "Nixon Ends Convertibility of US Dollars to Gold and Announces Wage/Price Controls" *Federal Reserve History* (Nov. 22, 2013) https://www.federalreservehistory.org/essays/gold_convertibility_ends

101   The primary lesson learned by American policymakers appears to be that permitting broad access to the news media to observe American military action is a huge mistake. Hence, reporters now tend to be "embedded" with American forces and policymakers believe that embedded reporters are more likely to report developments from war zones as officially desired.

102   It seems that protesters had a point; the affluent, the connected and the powerful were avoiding war service, while the poor and men of color could not avoid it. All three American US Presidents of Vietnam-era draft age, Bill Clinton, George W. Bush, and Donald Trump, all white men, managed to avoid "in-country" combat duty, two of them avoiding military service of *any* kind.

against rival empires. Although the Chinese, unlike the Americans, generally did not deploy their forces very far outside of their own borders, China was, and is, a major empire in its own right. The Soviets, of course, were also running an empire. When confronted with its own earlier, poor decisions, empires must make adjustments. Richard Nixon, despite his own efforts at escalating the Vietnam adventure in his first term, eventually became the champion of getting the hell out, on any terms.

Along the way, Nixon managed to correct two of the great idiocies of the post-war American empire by engaging both China and the Soviets. Nixon directly engaged Red China, the actual country of China rather than its capitalist exile stand-in on Taiwan. Partially because of Nixon's engagement in 1971, the People's Republic assumed China's UN Security Council seat and veto, and Taiwan became an "un-state," a strange status of *de facto* independence and sovereignty. Most countries officially pretend that Taiwan is just a "renegade province" of China because the People's Republic is really big and powerful.

Nixon resigned in August of 1974 from his self-inflicted Watergate scandal. By 1975, American forces and personnel left a collapsing Vietnam, some embarrassingly via helicopters from the Saigon embassy roof. To be sure, Americans are excellent at framing and internal propaganda. Most American school children are taught that the United States is a universal force for good, and that the Vietnam War was a misguided effort by an entirely beneficent nation that isn't an empire to protect the world from communist domination. After the Vietnam fiasco and after Watergate, the United States elected an actual career military officer, former submariner Jimmy Carter of Georgia. Carter, almost uniquely among American presidents, managed to avoid getting any military personnel killed in combat. He did lose military personnel in a failed hostage rescue effort in Iran, which itself resulted from his own failure at imperial management. Brutal autocrats called upon to serve as local American agents such as the Shah of Iran tend to be insanely unpopular among their own populations.

Carter's successor was Ronald Reagan of California. A competent movie actor, Reagan proved utterly brilliant as a propagandist as he set out to "restore American greatness." Somewhere along the way, Reagan literally gave us the line "make America great again," which would be recycled in the candidacy of Donald Trump. Reagan proceeded to undo any introspective measures Carter might have put in place, such as ripping solar panels from the White House roof lest Americans not try to burn as much non-renewable energy as possible just to show that we could. Reagan also proved that American military forces could win a decisive victory by decisively beating up the mighty Caribbean island of Grenada.

Reagan's successor, the affable patrician and former CIA Director, George H.W. Bush of Texas (actually from Connecticut), doubled down with a decisive victory against mighty Panama, capturing former American friend and later *persona non grata* Manuel Noriega. To his immense credit, H.W. Bush ably managed the international order amidst the implosion of one of the rival superpowers, the Soviet Union. By 1991, the USSR essentially placed a "going out of business" sign on itself, and emerged as the Russian Federation, plus about 15 other countries, in "the Commonwealth of Independent States;" the three Baltic republics of Latvia, Lithuania, and Estonia eventually wanted no part of this. As the Berlin Wall fell freeing East Germany from Soviet domination, soon to be joined by the entire communist bloc of the Warsaw Pact, H.W. Bush kept things orderly. [103]

A decade and a half of American military recovery from Vietnam abruptly ended with George H.W. Bush's decision to insert a massive number of American troops into the first Gulf War. Despite

---

[103] Unfortunately, his successor, Bill Clinton of Arkansas, would not be as orderly. Clinton foolishly expanded the American empire into most of the former Warsaw Pact. He did so as a matter of short-term domestic political advantage (*i.e.*, to woo Polish voters in Michigan and Ohio). Clinton did this at a time when the American empire was spent and could not easily absorb new vassals.

the overwhelming firepower brought to bear, although the vast "coalition of the willing" successfully removed Saddam Hussein's Iraqi forces from Kuwait, it could not remove Iraqi leader Saddam Hussein himself from power, and indeed, did not really try to do so.

The aftermath of the first Gulf War resulted in an ongoing encirclement of Iraq. The post-Gulf War order involved harsh sanctions on Iraq. As a result, observers concluded that this caused enormous suffering and the deaths of hundreds of thousands of vulnerable Iraqi citizens. [104] The Gulf War aftermath also required American forces at locations surrounding Iraq to maintain a "no-fly zone," including within the Kingdom of Saudi Arabia.

The placement of American troops within the Kingdom of Saudi Arabia was a problem for a number of reasons. For one, such a troop deployment would include women and Jews, neither of which were particularly welcome in "conservative" Saudi society. As a result, there was some unsurprising, and quite lethal, blowback.

In typical American fashion, the main blowback caused by George H.W. Bush's actions fell during his successor's term. Terrorism by Middle Easterners against American targets, which, despite propaganda conflating Israeli targets with American ones, had been only occasional. The Beirut US barracks bombing during the Reagan presidency [105] were a notable exception, but even there, the attack took place *in the Middle East.*

Terrorism against American targets became much more common during the term of Bill Clinton. Almost immediately after he took office, the first World Trade Center was bombed in February of 1993; this was followed by an attack on U.S. Air Force personnel at Khobar Towers (killing at least 19) in Saudi Arabia in 1996, the Nairobi, Kenya, and Dar-es-Salaam, Tanzania, American embassy bombings in 1998, and the USS Cole attack in Yemen in 2000. To be sure, there was also the Oklahoma City bombing by *American*

---

104   Crossette, Barbara, "Iraq Sanctions Kill Children, U.N. Reports," *The New York Times* (Dec. 1, 1995) https://www.nytimes.com/1995/12/01/world/iraq-sanctions-kill-children-un-reports.html

105   Glass, Andrew, "Reagan Condemns Beirut Bombing, October 23, 1983," *Politico* (Oct. 23, 2018) https://www.politico.com/story/2018/10/23/reagan-condemns-beirut-bombing-oct-23-1983-921655

terrorists against American civilians including quite a few *children* in 1995. Convicted terrorist Timothy McVeigh was the first federal prisoner executed in decades, that execution taking place just a few weeks before September 11, 2001.

For his part, Bill Clinton's ultimate response to being the first President to enter office in the post-Cold War world was to *immediately* try to get the Cold War party started again by expanding the American European colonization project, better known as "NATO," right up to the borders of Russia. By eventually including the former Soviet Baltic republics and a number of former Warsaw Pact members in the NATO alliance, Clinton was sowing the seeds for eventual trouble with a weakened, but hardly impotent, Russian state. At the same moment, Europe's first post-Cold War ground war spun out of control as the former Yugoslavia blew apart. Clinton's decision to bomb Belgrade, the capital of Serbia (then still called Yugoslavia) and Russia's only real ally in Europe, *really* amounted to something that would stick in Moscow's craw. [106] Nonetheless, perhaps because of the vaunted "peace dividend" or the internet bubble that bolstered the American economy, or perhaps even because of such politically calculated pandering such as his NATO expansions, Clinton actually remained popular at home despite the geopolitical hornets' nest he was opening with Russia.

Clinton's response to Middle Eastern troublemakers, particularly to the lethal twin bombings of American embassies in Nairobi, Kenya, and Dar-es-Salaam, Tanzania, by the shadowy Al-Qaeda group, was consistent with what most American presidents would do. He ordered the launching of some cruise missiles "somewhere,"

---

106   The bombing of Belgrade, which also included the "accidental" bombing of the Chinese embassy there, coincided in time with a rather mean-spirited domestic "situation" whereby the serial philanderers, Newt Gingrich, Bob Livingston, and others led their Republican Party to impeach Bill Clinton for having oral sex in the White House with intern Monica Lewinsky and then allegedly lying about it. Republicans impeached Clinton for supposed perjury, notwithstanding that his lawyers had engineered the definition of "sex" so that he actually *did not* lie about it during his legal troubles with Paula Jones. Although, *politician* Clinton took over for lawyer Clinton and *very blatantly did lie about it* to the American public. I only bring up the matter of the timing of the Belgrade bombing to observe just how far gone the American empire actually is. At critical, if not *existential,* moments when it should be planning the details of how it rules the world, the American empire instead concerns itself with debating the proposition that the President *might* have lied about getting a blow job.

to wit, a vitamin factory in Sudan, and a paramilitary training camp in Afghanistan. Bill Clinton would eventually prove to be the electoral death for his own wife's presidential ambitions, in no small part, because his NATO expansion inspired rival empire Russia to pull out all the stops to defeat her, as did her own actions as Secretary of State. Bill Clinton's own "issues" also proved too much for his earnest and experienced, albeit not exactly inspiring Vice President, Al Gore, to overcome in the 2000 election. Thus, despite Clinton's actual popularity and a reasonably strong economy, after just eight years of having had it with a president named George Bush, the American people welcomed another "George Bush." Many Americans, at least initially, thought it was just the old man giving it a second go. It was not the goofy but experienced old patrician, George H.W. Bush. Instead, 2000 saw the election of the son, George W. Bush. In a close and highly controversial election, with the help of a solid from a 5-4 U.S. Supreme Court majority, including alleged sexual harasser and George H.W. Bush nominee Clarence Thomas, Bush the Younger acquired the reins of the American empire.

Just as Bill Clinton had to deal with the blowback of his predecessor's actions in the first year of his presidency, George "Dubya" Bush got the mother of all blowbacks in his first year. After a few mostly inconsequential months in office, Dubya was met with a terrorist attack on the World Trade Center, only this one worked spectacularly. The 9/11 attacks took out both towers of the World Trade Center, one face of the Pentagon, and resulted in the deadly crash of an airliner in Shanksville, Pennsylvania. In all, the September 11th attacks caused almost 3,000 American deaths, making it the bloodiest day in the history of the United States "homeland" since the Civil War's Antietam battle in Maryland in the 1860s.

The opportunities to unleash violence presented by September 11th were not likely to go to waste in an administration that featured a number of signatories to the Project for a New American Century document, including Nixon-era holdovers Defense Secretary Donald

Rumsfeld, and Vice President Richard Bruce "Dick" Cheney. [107] Cheney and Rumsfeld set about ensnaring the United States into the military engagements that would ultimately lay waste to whatever life energy the American empire still had remaining to it.

A brief warm-up took place in Afghanistan. American forces began attacking that country in October of 2001. The early Afghan campaign was notable for letting Osama bin Laden escape, along with much of the leadership of Al-Qaeda. Al-Qaeda, of course, was the shadowy Wahabist/Islamist terrorist group linked to bin Laden and widely considered responsible for the earlier Nairobi and Dar-es-Salaam bombings, as well as the September 11th events. Ultimately, it was learned that bin Laden had escaped from Afghanistan into neighboring Pakistan (where he would remain under the apparent protection of the Pakistani military *living on the grounds of its military service academy* for about ten years, until his eventual execution at the hands of American Navy SEALs in 2011, followed by his entirely unsuspicious burial at sea). The early part of the Afghan conflict was also notable for the uncharacteristically visible and unusually nasty treatment of prisoners taken in the conflict. For various idiotic reasons, the Americans sent virtually every Arab man and many local Afghan and Pakistani nobodies to the American naval base at Guantanamo Bay in Cuba. Some prisoners were first tortured at "CIA black sites" before eventual transfer to Guantanamo. You will recall that the Americans acquired "GTMO" in the aftermath of the Spanish-American War. Then, as part of the Platt Amendment [108] by which the Americans maintained *de facto* control of Cuban affairs for a time, the US leased itself GTMO in perpetuity. As I write this in 2019, some 17 years after first holding prisoners there, forty men captured in the Afghan conflict, or at least "sort of" captured in the Afghan conflict, remain incarcerated there. These prisoners

107   *See* "Context of 'June 3, 1997: PNAC Think Tank Issues Statement of Principles,'" *History Commons* (retrieved June 16, 2019) http://www.historycommons.org/context.jsp?item=a060397pnacprinciples
108   Rothman, Lillian, "Why the United States Controls Guantanamo Bay," *Time* (Jan. 22, 2015) http://time.com/3672066/guantanamo-bay-history/

are held with no discernible end in sight perhaps remaining trapped there, most without charge, trial, or meaningful legal remedy, for the remainder of their own natural lives.

With a great deal of help from local warlords, the Taliban government in Afghanistan fell within a few weeks of the start of the American attacks there. With Afghanistan "successfully" behind it, Team Dubya turned toward its real target, oil-rich Iraq, concocting the soothing lie that Saddam Hussein had some responsibility for the September 11th attacks, a proposition the Bush Administration itself simultaneously debunked! More ominously, the Bush team argued that Saddam maintained an arsenal of WMDs (weapons of mass destruction), the ABCs of badness (atomic, biological, and chemical weapons). To hammer the point home, Team Dubya relied on two of its most publicly popular members, both of whom happened to be African-American. National Security Advisor Condoleezza Rice told us that we did not want Saddam's "smoking gun" to be "a mushroom cloud." And, in a move he personally regretted at the time and will likely regret for the rest of his life, Secretary of State Colin Powell pitched the United Nations Security Council with the threat posed by Saddam Hussein, complete with a tiny vial of something alleged to be a stand-in for chemical weapons.

Almost a year and a half to the day after September 11th, and shortly after chasing U.N. weapons inspectors out of Iraq, the United States began its war of ultimate national and imperial suicide with its "shock and awe" campaign in Baghdad, Iraq. As in Afghanistan, fast-moving American troops quickly routed the sitting government, and quickly ushered in a long, painful insurgency, an insurgency that has arguably never been fully resolved to this day.

The cost was extraordinary. Most economists and others who have assessed the various tolls associated with "the war on terror" have concluded that in addition to the thousands of *American* dead, tens of thousands or more egregiously wounded, plus other effects such as countless veterans' suicides, not to mention untold thousands of Iraqi and Afghan dead, the monetary cost alone was in the multi-

trillions of dollars. [109] These costs were incurred at a time when the US was already running massive deficits resulting from Republican tax cuts for the super-rich piled on top of the war spending.

An empire that never really recovered from the first Gulf War was ill-advised in getting itself stuck in a second one. Given the quite reasonable presumption that Messrs. Rumsfeld and Cheney were actually well aware that Saddam Hussein had no WMDs and of course, that he had nothing to do with September 11th, the purpose of the adventure quickly becomes clear. I would suggest that sometimes nomenclature is everything. The original name of the "Operation Iraqi Freedom" campaign in Iraq was, at least, according to two possible "slip-ups" by then White House press secretary Ari Fleischer, "Operation Iraqi Liberation" or "O.I.L." [110] In other words, the Dubya people, led by oil men Cheney and Bush, sought to deal with perceived future oil-supply problems by locking up Iraq's gigantic oil reserves thought to be the second or third largest in the world via military conquest. Simply put, I do not believe that either Rumsfeld or Cheney *was stupid enough to believe their own propaganda* about the threat of Islamist terrorism. So-called Islamist terrorism simply never presented the same kind of existential threat as Soviet (now Russian) nuclear ICBMs. Nonetheless, the extraordinary cost of the ultimate response to "the war on terror" seems to indicate that many policymakers thought it *actually might* be that kind of threat.

Unfortunately, George W. Bush's somewhat more intelligent successor, Barack Obama of Illinois, did not see fit to change many of the "war on terror" policies himself. Hence, the war in Afghanistan

---

109   A series of studies conducted by Brown University's Watson Institute for International and Public Affairs determined that American military actions in the so-called war on terror (now in over 80 countries) since September 11th have resulted in over 480,000 deaths directly attributable to fighting (including over 244,000 civilians). In addition, these operations have resulted in over 21 million displaced persons, numerous human rights abuses at every turn, and of course, a US Treasury monetary cost of *$5.9 trillion*. "Costs of War," *Watson Institute* (retrieved June 16, 2019) https://watson.brown.edu/costsofwar/

110   "The Iraq War was called 'Operation Iraqi Liberation' (OIL)?" *The Coincidence Theorist* (July 20, 2015) https://thecoincidencetheorist.com/political-corruption/the-iraq-war-was-called-operation-iraqi-liberation-oil/

raged on, albeit with a "surge," and then not. [111] The apparent lesson that Mr. Obama learned from Iraq and Afghanistan was simply "take no prisoners." Prisoners just become unfortunate "optics" when pictures of men in orange jumpsuits hit the press, so the best practice is not to take any. Even at the cost of lost intelligence opportunities, policy makers determined that it was just better to vaporize "insurgents" from remote-control drone aircraft than it would be to send boots on the ground to defeat or capture them. [112] The ultimate justification for such a brutal policy seems consistent with so much other short-term thinking: the technology to do so has improved dramatically. Put another way, the means justify the ends.

Remote-control drone warfare permits American war machines to operate in places like Yemen or Somalia where *other people* are having a raging war while the United States itself, officially at least, is not. Most importantly, if a drone fighter plane is shot down, the White House will not have to make annoying phone calls to the grieving families of service members, and newspapers will not print the names and pictures of casualties or show pictures of returning flag-draped coffins. The successor to Mr. Obama, a certain Mr. Donald Trump of New York, is delighted with having been handed the opportunity to use remote-control warfare, and he has directed "his generals" to step this up, and removed many of the "safeguards" on their use imposed by Mr. Obama. We have come to the late chapters of the American empire. After decades of outrageously high spending on military, security, and "intelligence" infrastructure at the expense of public civilian structure and a doctrinal aversion to any kind of national industrial policy, or indeed, *any* national policy other than slavery and foreign aggression, the United States has long since

---

111   Although "closing Guantanamo" was a set piece of Obama's campaign for the presidency, his continuation of the war in Afghanistan continued the principal legal excuse for maintaining the American US's showpiece gulag at Guantanamo, Cuba. Of course, his own Justice and Defense Departments fought most efforts to actually close the place and tightly held on to most of the prisoners they inherited until late in Obama's second term, when dozens of prisoners were released, some just a few days ahead of Donald Trump assuming office.

112   Zenko, Micah, "Obama's Embrace of Drone Strikes Will Be A Lasting Legacy," *The New York Times* (Jan. 12, 2016) https://www.nytimes.com/roomfordebate/2016/01/12/reflecting-on-obamas-presidency/obamas-embrace-of-drone-strikes-will-be-a-lasting-legacy

reached the point where its empire no longer pays for itself. Perhaps this is because it has already sucked the value out of everything. Whatever the reasons, thanks mostly to endless Republican tax cuts for the super-rich, the American empire no longer really pays *for much of anything* with real money, instead, borrowing or printing its way to a simulacrum of prosperity and security. Those alive today in the homeland of the American empire now subsidize an enterprise whose profitability and indeed viability other than for the recipients of the largesse of the national security state is shrinking fast. Still, heaven forbid that an American politician *ever* suggest reducing the defense budget.

Americans continue to enjoy their so-called Defense and Homeland Security budgets swallowing up most marginal dollars in the American economy as they "enjoy" the twilight of the American empire. And all that goes with it.

9. THE UNFAIR SEX

B EING AN AMERICAN WOMAN presents challenges that few other women on Earth face. At the outset, the United States has made it to *the list of the ten most dangerous countries on Earth for women,* an elite list which includes India, Afghanistan, Syria, Somalia, Saudi Arabia, Pakistan, Democratic Republic of Congo, Yemen, Nigeria, and *the United States.* [113] The other countries on this list are part of the "developing world" and are often war-torn, and are based in Asia and Africa. We have already alluded to some aspects of the "woman's paradise" presented by the United States, such as the United States' status as one of four countries—Swaziland, Lesotho, and Papua New Guinea, being the others—without mandatory paid maternity leave (*see* footnote 13). To be completely fair, the US is *also* the only developed country without any kind of mandated paid parental leave to men or to women. [114] This is still true at a time when women represent around 47% of the American workforce, and women represent around 52% of the so-called high-paying management, professional, and related occupations. [115] For good measure, women are vastly overrepresented

---

113   "Experts say U.S. among 10 most dangerous nations for women," *CBS News* (June 26, 2018) https://www.cbsnews.com/news/us-10-most-dangerous-country-for-women-thompson-reuters-survey-amid-metoo/
114   Livingston, Gretchen, "Among 41 Nations, U.S. Is the Outlier When it comes to paid parental leave," *Fact Tank, Pew Research Center* (Sep. 26, 2016) http://www.pewresearch.org/fact-tank/2016/09/26/u-s-lacks-mandated-paid-parental-leave/
115   "Women in the Labor Force in 2010," *U.S. Department of Labor, Women's Bureau* (retrieved June 9, 2019) https://www.dol.gov/wb/factsheets/qf-laborforce-10.htm

among American college graduates. Women are the recipients of 61.6% of all associate's degrees granted in a recent year, 56.7% of all bachelor's degrees, 59.9% of all master's degrees, and 51.6% of all doctorate degrees. [116] Nonetheless, American women's earnings remain stuck at only around 81% of men's earnings.

One might assume that this outsized level of educational achievement by women means that women will inevitably reach the highest rungs of corporate America and the American power structure. This has not happened. Barely 5% of corporate leaders are women, as are barely 20% of corporate board members. As I write this in 2019, there has never been a female American President or Vice President, and less than 20% of American legislators are female. [117] It is appropriate to discuss the treatment of children in the United States in the context of women, because Americans tend to assume that women are in charge of raising them. We start our observation by examining the remarkably high costs of child care compared to other places. Estimates are that an American single parent pays an inconceivable 52% of their income on child care costs, and a couple pays about a quarter of their family income, compared to 10-15% of household income or less paid in most other industrialized countries. [118] The American child poverty rate of about 23% puts the United States in 34th place worldwide and the worst in the so-called "developed" world. [119] Admittedly, this is a relatively small survey, and to be fair, the US is actually 34th *out of 35* developed countries. In your face, Romania! The rubber *really* hits the road in terms of American treatment of women in the area of women's health care and reproductive "rights," a subject we have brushed upon before.

---

116   Kirst, Michael W., "Women Earn More Degrees than Men; Gap Keeps Increasing," *Stanford/The College Puzzle* (May 18, 2013) https://collegepuzzle.stanford.edu/tag/women-exceed-men-in-college-graduation/

117   Brown, Anna, "Despite gains, women remain underrepresented among U.S. political and business leaders," *Fact Tank, Pew Research Center* (Mar. 20, 2017) https://www.pewresearch.org/fact-tank/2017/03/20/despite-gains-women-remain-underrepresented-among-u-s-political-and-business-leaders/

118   Howard, Jaqueline, "The costs of child care around the world," *CNN.com* (Apr. 25, 2018) https://www.cnn.com/2018/04/25/health/child-care-parenting-explainer-intl/index.html

119   Garofalo, Pat, "Report: US Has One Of The Highest Child Poverty Rates In The Developed World, *Think Progress* (May 29, 2012) https://thinkprogress.org/report-us-has-one-of-the-highest-child-poverty-rates-in-the-developed-world-c43e3f4b5da1/

Although the right to obtain an abortion became an American constitutional right in 1973, when the *Roe v. Wade* decision was issued by the Supreme Court, many American states are preparing for the day (perhaps soon) when a right-wing Supreme Court will change that. At least thirteen states have passed laws that would *immediately* criminalize abortion if *Roe* were overturned. [120] Even with *Roe* still the law of the land, anecdotal evidence is that over 87% of American counties lack so much as a single abortion provider. [121]

Meanwhile, the current American government appears to be trying to reduce women's access to *contraceptive products.* [122]

Let us conclude this discussion with a simple thought exercise. Had the more than 50 million legal abortions, the estimated number performed between *Roe* and 2008, [123] not taken place, tens of millions of then-unwanted children would have been born. They, in turn, would have flooded American labor roles, further overcrowded American schools and prisons, and, of course, served as a highly useful surplus labor force that the US could have used to suppress wages even faster than automation, outsourcing, and exploiting undocumented immigrant labor.

In the American context, the "right to life" is certainly about keeping women in a vulnerable and subservient role. It also has a macro-element. Like all other American issues, it seems to be most fundamentally about ostensible *slavery* and reducing any potential power of the American worker to challenge his or her capitalist betters.

---

120   Tatham, Chelsea, "These states would automatically outlaw abortion if *Roe v. Wade* is overturned," *WTSP.com* (Mar. 19, 2019) https://www.wtsp.com/article/news/politics/these-states-would-automatically-outlaw-abortion-if-roe-v-wade-is-overturned/67-05711c8f-e7cb-4364-b217-5e787dff9420

121   Weiner, Rachel, "No Choice: 87% of U.S. Counties Have No Access To Abortion Clinic, *HuffPost* (Dec. 6, 2017) https://www.huffingtonpost.com/2009/06/02/no-choice-87-of-us-counti_n_210194.html

122   "Editorial: Stop Trump rules blocking access to contraceptives," *Tampa Bay Times* (Jan. 2, 2019) http://www.tampabay.com/opinion/editorials/editorial-stop-trump-rules-blocking-access-to-contraceptives-20190102/

123   Jones, Rachel K. and Kooistra, Kathryn, "Abortion Incidence and Access to Services In the United States, 2008," *Perspectives on Sexual and Reproductive Health, Guttmacher Inst.* (March 2011) https://www.guttmacher.org/sites/default/files/pdfs/pubs/journals/4304111.pdf

10. NERVOUS NELLIES

THE UNITED STATES IS *NUMBER one in the world* with a staggering 18% of its adult population enjoying anxiety disorders each year. [124] To some extent, this is actually a good sign. It means that there are at least some Americans, around one in five at any given time, *conscious enough* to realize just how badly their own nation "functions." Indian philosopher Jidda Krishnamurti famously observed, "It is no measure of health to be well adjusted to a profoundly sick society."

Nonetheless, American propaganda also remains second to none; the Soviet Union could have used some lessons from it. George Orwell and Aldous Huxley anticipated *some* of the technical advances in mind control that Americans currently enjoy. However, those great visionaries of dystopia also anticipated *some* level of social resistance that would ultimately necessitate brute force. For the most part, the American empire has actually not had to employ much force on its own people to quell political opposition, at least not yet. Orwell and Huxley could not have envisioned hundreds of millions of people all over the world *voluntarily handing over virtually every aspect of their own identity and existence* to profit-making companies. These profit-making companies, in turn, sell the data to other profit-making companies, and of course, to the American security state. As we learned in the aftermath of the

---

124   Ducharme, Jamie, "A Lot of Americans Are More Anxious Than They Were Last Year, A New Poll Says," *Time* (May 8, 2018) https://time.com/5269371/americans-anxiety-poll/

2016 national election, these same profit-making companies have no problem selling the very same data to *hostile* nations' security services, too! In America, everything is for sale. Under the present version of American capitalism, all Americans are now capitalists who are more than willing to sell the rope by which to hang themselves.

The "upside" of the hilariously named "social media" is that "the user" receives, usually "for free," an efficient platform for the viewing of other people's photos of their vacations, meals, and pets. This process achieves the salutary purpose for the American system and capitalism, anyway of ensuring that most "social media" participants remain mired in feelings of hopelessness and blissful inadequacy. This is because one's "friends" are leading lives so much more wonderful than they are, at least, according to the pictures. The fact that virtually everything posted on social media seems posed (if not fraudulent) is irrelevant: so many pictures! As alleged former Soviet national Yakov Smirnov would yet again say, "America, what a country!" American capitalism always finds a way. Just as the United States is number one in anxiety disorders, it is also number one for the use of antidepressant medications, and indeed, for pretty much all medications. One would assume that, at some point, these numerous medications would "kick in," and serve to eventually reduce the incidence of mental health problems, or at least reduce the incidence of *some* medical problems. One would assume incorrectly. Indeed, this would represent a profound misunderstanding of the American health care system.

Before we discuss more precisely what is wrong with the American health care sector and, in particular, why insanely expensive medicines and treatments often fail to "make anyone better," at least in the aggregate sense of overall American public health, we will take a brief diversion into economics. We must first understand the peculiarly absurd way in which Americans conduct their national accounting. A typical high school or college economics course will introduce students to the concept of "Gross Domestic Product" or "GDP." We learn that GDP is the cumulative total of all the goods and services bought and sold in a given economic entity, usually an independent nation state. For the year 2018, American GDP was around $20 trillion. [125] Per capita GDP can be calculated simply by dividing that GDP number by the officially 327 million people in the American population, and we come up with an average of about $61,000 in per capita GDP. Officially, the US sports a median household income, as measured for 2013-2017, of between $57,000 and $58,000. [126] This means that around half the households are above that, and half are below. The reason why *per capita* average income is higher than *median household income* is because a few people at the top of the American pyramid, *the people for whom the system is designed,* have extremely high incomes, which skews the difference between "median household" and "average *per capita.*" The harsh reality is that something like 80% of Americans live paycheck to paycheck with limited savings, and crippling debt. We will discuss this further a bit later. I take you on this diversion to economics in a discussion of health care because, of course, the purpose for how the United States conducts its GDP accounting is to make sure that the gross numbers go up, preferably every single year. This way, the nation's politicians can take credit for "growth" even at the price of *everyone in the country being profoundly and hopelessly miserable.* Indeed, American economic growth has historically been very strong. Strong growth has in turn attracted business and immigrants, lather, rinse, repeat.

Slower economic growth, now the case *for decades,* has exposed the American system as being the actual hell-scape that it is. The American system can no longer paper over its unique horrors while it suffers *a failing* economy. Such horrors include a complete lack of a meaningful culture or institutions of support for the less well-off, other than "charitable" institutions, often religious-based, whose mission seems to be as much about the *shaming* of those

---

125   "GDP Grows 2.9% in United States," *Country Economy* (retrieved June 17, 2019) https://countryeconomy.com/gdp/usa?year=2018
126   "Quick Facts - United States," *United States Census* Bureau, (retrieved June 17, 2019) https://www.census.gov/quickfacts/fact/table/US/HSD410217

on the short end of capitalism's stick as it is about assisting them. Indeed, there is an apparent paucity of cultural values for *anything* besides economic prosperity. Stripped of the one thing that the US traditionally had going for it, one can see why many people would be "anxious" or worse. In other words, it's not you; it's just America, being America.

Idyllic but not particularly economically developed places like the Himalayan kingdom of Bhutan tout a "gross domestic happiness" index. [127] I suspect that if the reverse measure were undertaken, a gross domestic *unhappiness* index, the United States would take its rightful place as the number one unhappiest place on Earth, particularly if measured in a *non-fraudulent* way. Accounting is quite relevant to our discussion of American anxiety disorders and the other "successes" of American health care because the American method of GDP accounting uses an entirely "value-neutral" method: all transactions are added up by their dollar value. Hence, the kale farmer earning a dollar gets the same accounting as the tobacco farmer earning a dollar as does the anti-tobacco campaigner receiving a dollar in funding.

The harsh reality is that, to run up GDP numbers, keeping people in a state of "un-health" has proven far more profitable for the big *kahunas* of health care (that would be "Big Pharma," "Big Insurance," hospitals, and to a lesser extent, the professional practitioners such as physicians, dentists and the like) than keeping people healthy would. For just one example of how this operates, we observe that the care and treatment for *the single condition* of diabetes was estimated to "cost $327 *billion*" in 2017 in the United States. [128] Let me repeat that: treating one condition represents almost 2% of the world's largest GDP.

Of this staggering sum, however, "only" $90 billion represents

---

127   Kelly, Annie, "Gross national happiness in Bhutan: the big idea from a tiny state that could change the world," *The Guardian* (Dec. 1, 2012) https://www.theguardian.com/world/2012/dec/01/bhutan-wealth-happiness-counts

128   Cryts, Aine, "The Biggest Barrier to Home Health Care," *Managed Health Care Executive* (Feb. 1, 2019) https://www.managedhealth careexecutive.com/member-engagement/biggest-barrier-home-health care

"lost productivity," that is, sick time from work and lost revenue or "productivity" as a result, money that likely *will not* be added to GDP because it does not represent a transfer of goods and services that can be easily measured. The remaining $237 billion, well over 1% of the American GDP, *can* be measured. It represents the "direct costs" of drugs and other medical treatments for diabetes.

In a rational society, of course, *all of these costs* would be regarded as a catastrophic drag on the economy. A rational society might even declare a national emergency and implement remedial measures to address the diabetes crisis, such as a crash national diet and exercise program starting in schools and work places. In the case of diabetes, however, the American "health care" system views the condition as a *humongous profit opportunity*. Hence, American national account keepers *do not* deduct the more than $200 billion in treatment costs from national GDP as the dead weight it is, as a more rational country might. Instead, American account keepers *add it* to national income, as if it were equivalent to an investment in plant and equipment.

Indeed, so far gone is American understanding of this basic principle of economics that no less a figure than Nobel Laureate in Economics, Paul Krugman, has suggested that the American economy could *benefit mightily* from an extraterrestrial alien invasion. [129] This would of course result in massive levels of mayhem and destruction. Nonetheless, such an invasion would also result in ramping-up military spending for "defense" and of course, it would require a massive infusion of mostly public money for armaments, transport of troops, and everything that goes with a good war. Perhaps just as importantly, there would be massive spending after the alien invasion and war on reconstruction projects. Thus, the alien invasion would (wait for it) *stimulate the economy.*

Perhaps my own lack of a Nobel Prize in economics makes me dubious as to this analysis. It seems to me that the vast amounts

---

129   Sanburn, Josh, "Paul Krugman: An Alien Invasion Could Fix the Economy," *Time,* (Aug. 16, 2011) http://business.time.com/2011/08/16/paul-krugman-an-alien-invasion-could-fix-the-economy/

of money for war and reconstruction, while perhaps capable of *locally* stimulating the regions that house defense contractors and areas being reconstructed, *must come from somewhere else* in the economy. In other words, the so-called free market might have made "more productive allocations" of money, such as investing in research and development or for new plants and equipment or for training or education. Once the alien onslaught begins, however, money *must* be spent on defense and on rebuilding things that had *already been there before.* My non-Nobel Laureate mind sees that this is bad...society and the economy as a whole are ultimately *less* well off, even if certain defense contractors and construction contractors make out like bandits. How, you might rightly ask, does *any of this* relate to American health care and GDP let alone the extraordinary levels of American anxiety that this chapter is supposed to be discussing? I am suggesting that most expenditures on health care should be considered a drag on rather than a boon to the economy as a whole. [130] Like having to rebuild a city that was already there before, expensive efforts to recover the lost health of a previously healthy person should be deemed economic dead weight.

This is just not how Americans roll. The polar opposite of how Americans deal with health care may be found in the traditional economic model for Chinese medicine. In that model, one regularly seeks out consultation with a medical practitioner—presumably far more often than the annual check-up that Americans are supposed to get but most don't. The friendly medical practitioner performs an examination, and then prescribes herbs and other "lifestyle" remedies, perhaps a recommended diet or physical movement plan. Then the patient pays the fee *as long as the patient remains healthy.* [131] If one's health fails, they do not pay the practitioner, because, of course, they have been failed. Measures taken by the practitioner to

---

130   Exceptions to this method of accounting could be made for medical research and development or for hospital construction, for example, or services related to "maintaining health" as opposed to "treating illness."

131   "What if you only paid doctors when you were healthy?" *SeaGate World* (June 13, 2015) http://www.seagateworld.com/2015/06/western-medicine-get-paid-when-you-get-sick/

restore one to health are at his or her expense and not the patient's. This entirely rational approach that incentivizes good health is the precise *mirror opposite* of how American health care operates. American health care incentivizes *profit* at every turn, sometimes even in a seemingly never-ending *Munchausen syndrome by proxy* scenario of making patients sick as part of the effort to cure them!

To be sure, sound nutritional practices such as a diet of sustainable and wholesome foods, and the use of exercise clubs and health spas and similar facilities *could* be very profitable in their own right and often are. Indeed, such practices might be the mainstays of health care spending in a different system, one whose fundamental organizational principle is based on something *other* than maintaining ostensible *slavery*. [132] The American model has allowed the meteoric growth of some of the world's largest and most profitable corporations found within "Big Pharma." These entities are often the star performers in many Americans' pension funds or individual retirement plans. Their public relations departments will tell you that these drug companies spend enormous sums of money developing the exciting new blockbuster, lifesaving drugs in their state-of-the-art laboratories for the good of humanity. The more mundane reality is that much of the actual research and development of pharmaceuticals is performed in government laboratories, or in public or private universities mostly at government expense. On the other hand, the *benefits* of the research are frequently handed over, often for free, to Big Pharma. Only then will the major drug companies manufacture the new "wonder drug," and then mark it up at unconscionably high levels, often claiming intellectual property protection for something that had been developed at government expense. The dysfunction of this particular arrangement is best

---

132   Indeed, it is difficult to imagine a more dystopian arrangement than an unhealthy American made hopelessly addicted to an expensive medicine that he or she can only afford through the health insurance that their employer provides—if he or she can afford it at all. It is not hard to imagine that such an American actually hates their job, but can't risk changing it (and losing that health insurance). Nor can they wean themselves from the medicine because it is simultaneously making them sick and making them addicted to it. I suggest, however, that millions of Americans routinely find themselves in this position.

demonstrated by the fact that Big Pharma spends far more on marketing and advertising than it does on research and development. [133]

Historically, the marketing of pharmaceutical products in the United States was "expert to expert." Pharmaceutical companies dispatched credentialed expert sales personnel to individual medical practitioners, and briefed them with free samples, and perhaps, the occasional dinner or trip to Hawaii on the benefits of their particular new wonder drug. These "detail men" (and detail women) would "educate" practitioners on why it would be beneficial to their patients to increase the number of prescriptions written for "WhamBammo" or whatever wonder drug was on offer. This arrangement was profitable and actually sustainable for all concerned. Nonetheless, Big Pharma realized that there was a way that it could *really* step up the promotion of its products—some of them highly addictive. Thus, the US joined only otherwise rational New Zealand in permitting television advertising for *prescribed* pharmaceutical products. [134] The race to hell has been on ever since! The genius of this arrangement now encourages even people who are not hypochondriacs to confront their medical practitioners and demand that they be prescribed WhamBammo for their psoriasis or acne, notwithstanding that the "label use" might be for high blood pressure.

Whether or not the advent of direct television advertising has increased Big Pharma's profits, Big Pharma certainly believes in television advertising, and is doing more of it. [135] Ironically, particularly as Big Pharma advertises to an ever older and sicker audience (after all, who still watches *television*?), the reading of a

---

133   *See, e.g.,* Eichler, Alexander, "Pharmaceutical Companies Spent 19 times More on Self-Promotion Than Basic Research: Report," *HuffPost* (May 8, 2013) https://www.huffpost.com/entry/pharmaceutical-companies-marketing_n_1760380
134   Lazarus, David, "Direct to Consumer Drug Sales," A Bad Idea that's Only Going to Get Worse," *Los Angeles Times* (Feb. 15, 2017) https://www.latimes.com/business/la-fi-lazarus-drugadvertising-20170215-story.html
135   Kaufman, Joanne, "Think You're Seeing More Drug Ads on TV? You Are, and Here's Why," *The New York Times* (Dec. 24, 2017) https://www.nytimes.com/2017/12/24/business/media/prescription-drugs-advertising-tv.html

lengthy list of horrific side effects actually makes the adverts *more credible*! You might rightly ask, once the new and exciting wonder drug cures you of your ills and you resume your good health, what will Big Pharma do for an encore? Of course, if you are asking such questions, you very likely do not understand the American health care system.

Some have asked the musical question, "Why Aren't Americans Healthier?" [136] The conclusion reached is that the American system's lack of social spending on *almost anything* before people get very sick, such as on food or housing subsidies that might reduce stress and other factors that contribute to illness, followed by its insistence on *massive spending* on treating the resultant illness, might be somewhat "counterproductive." Other issues that lead to the American health "situation" include social and economic disparities, high rates of obesity, risky behaviors, and, of course, a substantial uninsured population.

On the other hand, access to pharmaceuticals has never been higher as more Americans regularly take prescription drugs than ever before, with some estimates suggesting that over 50% of adults regularly take pharmaceuticals and many people taking *four or more*. [137]

Other reports suggest that the number of American adults who regularly take prescription drugs is more like *70%*. [138] Then again, still further studies show that millions of Americans do not take the drugs prescribed for them *because of their excessive cost*. [139] The high cost of pharmaceuticals and the fact that all out-of-pocket "health care" costs are beyond the reach of millions of people is just

---

136   Pomerance Berl, Rachel, "Why Aren't Americans Healthier?" *U.S. News & World Report* (Jan. 15, 2013) https://health.usnews.com/health-news/articles/2013/01/15/why-arent-americans-healthier

137   Preidt, Robert, Americans Taking More Prescription Drugs Than Ever: Survey," *HealthDay* (Aug. 3, 2017) https://consumer.healthday.com/general-health-information-16/prescription-drug-news-551/americans-taking-more-prescription-drugs-than-ever-survey-725208.html

138   "Study shows 70% of Americans take prescription drugs," *CBS News* (June 20, 2013) https://www.cbsnews.com/news/study-shows-70-percent-of-americans-take-prescription-drugs/

139   LeWine, Howard, "Millions of adults skip medications due to their high cost," *Harvard Health Publishing (Harvard Med. Sch.)* (Jan. 30, 2015) https://www.health.harvard.edu/blog/millions-skip-medications-due-to-their-high-cost-201501307673

one of many problems with American "health insurance." There are numerous others. [140]

One might suggest that infusion of pharmaceuticals into the American population has not greatly improved the metrics of "health." Of course, one could say that about the massive infusions of *money* into the health care industrial complex. Ah, but you, Dear Reader, are clever enough to know that the American model of *everything* remains ostensible *slavery*. Hence, nothing could possibly be as simple as what I have just described, and kudos to you, because you have caught me!

The brilliance of tying "health insurance" to employment in the American system has proven to be a win-win in *so many* ways that I am sure to miss most of them! First, of course, is that once someone finds a job with health insurance, and many jobs still do not come with health insurance, which explains, for example, why millions of people on Medicaid *actually have jobs*, it is that much harder to ever leave that job. [141] The health insurance will continue only as long as one maintains either that job, or at least maintains employment with that organization. If one were to leave the job, whether because they foolishly think they are *not* a slave, or perhaps because the employer wants to *remind them* that they really are a slave and duly sacks them, or even because they choose to change the *form* of slavery from one job to another, they will lose their health insurance. If this happens, they must purchase benefits through the wonderfully named program called "COBRA." [142] The venomously high premiums will probably kill the slave at the exact same moment that they have lost income from the job that they no longer have!

Next we consider the actual cost of health insurance itself. Among the reasons why Americans' paychecks have remained flat,

140   Kliff, Sarah, "8 facts that explain what's wrong with American health care," *Vox.com* (Jan. 20, 2015) https://www.vox.com/2014/9/2/6089693/health-care-facts-whats-wrong-american-insurance
141   Luhby, Tami, "Millions of Medicaid Recipients Already Work," *CNN* (Jan. 10, 2018) https://money.cnn.com/2018/01/10/news/economy/medicaid-work-requirement/index.html
142   COBRA (Consolidated Omnibus Reconciliation Act of 1986) is the federal law that allows people to keep health insurance after leaving a job; if an employee or a family member recently left a job with group health insurance, they may be able to continue this coverage by paying the *full cost* of the insurance.

or in real terms, declined over the last several years or even decades has been the steep rise in the cost to employers of providing health insurance. [143] Although many employers have attempted to slough off some or all health insurance costs onto their employees, even this gets harder to do when wages are flat or even declining. And many Americans are often surprised, in a very bad way, to find that the health coverage premiums that more or less bankrupt them every month might well *actually bankrupt them again* should they actually get sick and need "coverage." This is because their insurer may well refuse to pay for treatment, and force the "insured" to fight for benefits, possibly in court, with no assurance of obtaining coverage. In such a ludicrous system, it is hardly surprising that *medical debt is a major factor in American personal bankruptcies.* [144] Ironically, in most cases, those seeking bankruptcy protection with medical debts involved *actually have* some kind of "health insurance."

One of the main reasons for the denial of coverage used to be the exclusion for "pre-existing conditions." This is an artifact of the "insurance" concept: one should not be able to stick the *100 % certainty* of a cost one knows is coming onto a third-party insurer who is trying to *manage risk*. By analogy, the ideal time to buy fire insurance is just as your house is burning down. Despite the business necessity for this practice, if we are to believe health insurance is actually insurance at all, this particular exclusion was extremely unpopular with consumers.

So-called "Obamacare" put a limit on insurance companies' ability to exclude pre-existing conditions. Nonetheless, capitalism always finds a way. As insurers must cover more medical services by law, they have raised "deductibles" and "co-payments" (the cash one must pay the medical provider *in addition* to what the insurer will pay) and limited the number of service providers for whom they

---

143   "Why Health Care Eats More Of Your Paycheck Every Year," *NBC* News (Nov. 4, 2016) https://www.nbcnews.com/health/health-news/why-health-care-eats-more-your-paycheck-every-year-n678051
144   Mangan, Dan, "Medical Bills Are the Biggest Cause of US Bankruptcies, Study," *CNBC* (July 24, 2013) https://www.cnbc.com/id/100840148

will even provide coverage. Depending on the rapaciousness of the health care provider involved, and how miserly the health insurer is, the deductible and co-payment might exceed what the insurer will actually pay; in such event, the medical debt could become so large that it causes bankruptcy. This is not remotely farfetched: it actually happens in the United States *hundreds of thousands of times a year.*

The delicious win-win nature of the glorious American system is almost on full display here! Unless one is eligible for either or both of the two Great Society health programs based on poverty (Medicaid) or old age (Medicare), one must hold down a job whether they like it or not just to have health insurance, or otherwise they must pay an astronomically high premium for individual coverage. [145] If one did not have health insurance, "Obamacare" imposed a tax penalty, although "Trumpcare" changed that, just as it changed many other features of "Obamacare" in a package far too complicated for this general discussion. If one is self-employed, or works for an employer that "shares" the cost of health care with employees, a significant part of one's pay might go to pay the health insurance premium. If the employee or a member of their family actually does get sick, the uninsured portion of the medical expense *could be so financially devastating as to result in bankruptcy!* Satan himself could not have designed a more convoluted or dystopian system, or presumably, *a more profitable one.*

For their part, the denizens of "Big Pharma" think nothing of astronomically raising their drug prices regularly, sometimes every year, knowing that most of it will probably be borne by insurers, including governmental insurers. Those unfortunates who must pay out of pocket can just go ahead and go bankrupt, or just die!

For their part, American hospitals are notoriously the best in the world at hiding their prices *for everything* until one gets a mysterious invoice. Indeed, many hospitals seem entirely incapable

---

145   "Obamacare" did provide a subsidy for purchase of private health insurance based on meeting certain income limits. Undoing this has been the subject of much effort of the current American government in what it calls "Trumpcare."

of telling you the prices of their own services until issuing an invoice. That invoice, in turn, will be "discounted heavily," and an insurance company may only pay a tiny fraction of it anyway; still, the decision of whether to bankrupt a patient and their family often turns on an arbitrary dance between the faceless bureaucrats of a hospital billing department and a health insurer.

All told, it really is hard to think of a more Kafkaesque or dystopian nightmare scenario than getting sick in America. From the lair of his own dystopian nightmare in Branson, Missouri, former alleged Soviet citizen, Yakov Smirnov, might well say it best: "America, what a country!" In such a "health care" system, incidence of anxiety disorders at a mere one in five of the American population seems low!

11. Guns Blazing

THE SECOND AMENDMENT TO THE United States Constitution states: "A well-regulated Militia, being necessary to the security of a free State, the right of the people to keep and bear Arms, shall not be infringed."

A rational person would interpret this as being "structural," *i.e.*, a "there *shall* be" kind of clause, like "there shall be a President and a Supreme Court," there shall be *militias* in order to provide for common defense functions for the nation-state. *No rational person* would interpret this provision as a *"thou shalt not"* clause banning the regulation of firearms. "Rational person" tends to be entirely inconsistent with "American citizen" of course. Even a figure as committed to keeping Americans as backward thinking as the late Supreme Court Justice Antonin Scalia recognized that the Second Amendment doesn't necessarily prevent *all* "reasonable regulation" of firearms, such as keeping military-assault weapons with automatic-firing mechanisms out of the hands of adjudicated psychopaths. [146] Thus, it remains impressive that a tiny minority of the extreme right-wing controls the gun game.

The rationale for American gun policy is simply that *gunz are kewl*. Plus, the Russian-backed National Rifle Association has some really kickass lobbyists. Hence, goes the absurd rationale, the government shouldn't do *anything* to stop the occasional white male

---

146   *See e.g., District of Columbia v. Heller*, 554 U.S. 570 (2008)

(*always* white and *always* male) from shooting up a school, a movie theater, a work place, a house of worship, or just, you know, any place except where the actual moneyed elite might be found. We will try to avoid discussing the actual rationale for American gun policy, *i.e.,* widespread gun ownership, especially among white males, is an extremely effective *force-multiplier for oligarchy.* The fact that American Exceptionalism deliberately empowers millions of white males with a stake *in the racial hierarchy status quo* by arming them is a discussion that would probably be too disturbing to have. Instead, we will just discuss a few facts and statistics. In the area of personal firearms ownership, the United States is number one, in this case, "with a bullet." [147] In raw terms, the US sports almost 400 million firearms in private hands for its nearly 330 million people, translating to a world leading 120 guns per 100 people. By God, do Americans *use* their guns. According to one study of 22 leading industrialized countries, the US, with half of the population of the other 22 countries in the study, nonetheless accounted for 82% of all of the gun deaths. [148] The US, as we know, proudly in the top-ten-most-dangerous-countries-for-women, accounted for 90% of all women killed by guns. And 91% *of children under 14* who died by gun violence were in the United States. Further, the same study found that 92% of the young people between ages 15 and 24 killed by guns were also in the good old US.

There is a famous statistic trotted out, usually every December. As Comrade Stalin said, "a single death is a tragedy, a million deaths is a statistic." Since John Lennon was murdered in 1980, over a million Americans have been killed by firearms. [149] You might rightly conclude that anything even approaching a *healthy* or even a *sane* country would have put a stop to this a long, long time ago. As

147   "Estimated number of civilian guns per capita by country," *Wikipedia* (retrieved June 9, 2019) https://en.wikipedia.org/wiki/Estimated_number_of_civilian_guns_per_capita_by_country
148   Preidt, Robert, "How U.S. gun deaths compare to other countries," *CBS News* (Feb. 3, 2016) https://www.cbsnews.com/news/how-u-s-gun-deaths-compare-to-other-countries/
149   Stuart, Tessa, "1.15 Million Americans Have Been Killed by Guns Since John Lennon's Death," *Rolling Stone* (Dec. 8, 2015) https://www.rollingstone.com/politics/politics-news/1-15-million-americans-have-been-killed-by-guns-since-john-lennons-death-43117/

you have no doubt concluded by now, the US is neither a sane nor a healthy country. To be sure, only a minority of Americans have firearms in their homes, roughly a third or so, meaning that whoever *has* guns has *a lot of them.* [150] Although believed to be necessary "for safety," in the United States, guns are far more likely to be used on their owners or a member of the owner's family than upon anyone else. [151] Although the damage that military-style assault weapons have caused is devastating in scale, and even though only a small minority of gun owners have them, there are still *millions* of such weapons in the hands of American civilians. [152] These military-style assault weapons, routinely permitted in the hands of civilians *in a country where 18% of the population suffers anxiety disorders and might or might not be on anti-anxiety medication at any moment,* often feature prominently in the mass shootings that Americans now "enjoy" at the rate of more than one *per day.* [153]

Although the American right-wing rails endlessly about "abortion on demand" as a matter of being "pro-life," it is politically "mainstream" *among the very same people* to steadfastly oppose *any regulation* of firearms at all. This position holds firm even among office-holders even as over 90% of the American public favors such regulation as universal background checks for gun owners, [154] *i.e.*, persons adjudged insane or criminals or other "risky" persons, domestic violence suspects, for example, should not be permitted to own or possess firearms. Of course, neither the federal government nor a great many American states have any interest in anything of

---

150   Morin, Rich, "The demographics and politics of gun owning households," *Fact Tank, Pew Research Center* (July 14, 2014) https://www.pewresearch.org/fact-tank/2014/07/15/the-demographics-and-politics-of-gun-owning-households/
151   "The Person You're Most Likely To Kill With Your Gun Is You," *National Memo* (Dec. 19, 2012) https://www.nationalmemo.com/the-person-youre-most-likely-to-kill-with-your-gun-is-you/
152   Schoen, John W., "Owned by 5 million Americans, AR-15 under renewed fire after Orlando massacre," *CNBC* (June 13, 2016) https://www.cnbc.com/2016/06/13/owned-by-5-million-americans-ar-15-under-renewed-fire-after-orlando-massacre.html
153   Santhanam, Laura and Crigger, Megan, "More than one mass shooting happens per day in U.S., data shows," *PBS News Hour* (Oct. 2, 2015) https://www.pbs.org/newshour/nation/one-mass-shooting-happens-per-day-u-s-data-shows
154   Kirtscher, Tom, "A mostly on target claim: 97 percent of gun owners support universal background checks," *PolitiFact Wisconsin* (Mar. 2, 2018) https://www.politifact.com/wisconsin/statements/2018/mar/02/tammy-baldwin/mostly-target-claim-97-percent-gun-owners-support-/

the kind, even if the statistics show significant improvements in reducing violence. For example, states with universal background checks have 15% fewer homicides than states that do not. [155]

With respect to guns, however, facts just do not matter to Americans. Nor have they ever really mattered. This is because of guns' unique place in the organizing DNA of America. Access to firearms has been one of the few areas in which the feudal lords granted the *white* peasants any modicum of power. Indeed, bearing arms is the single-most jealously guarded "right" that non-elite Americans hold.

In colonial times and in the early days of the republic, the United States was spread out and almost entirely agrarian and rural. In such an environment, firearms were used for hunting for food or for repulsing rampaging animals threatening the established farm or livestock on it. Being spread out and rural, the assistance of a constabulary in the pre-telecommunications days would be extremely unlikely in the event of a rampaging neighbor or interloper, or of course, in the event that Native peoples irritated by being dispossessed from their rightful land might appear every now and again. All of which presented a very useful suite of uses for firearms. [156] This state of affairs persisted more or less into the 20th century, when the forces of urbanization brought large numbers of people into the large American cities from the countryside. Eventually, as a critical mass of people coming to the cities were people of color, urbanization patterns "reversed" and large numbers of white people moved out of the cities and into the peculiarly American dystopian nightmare called the "suburbs;" we will discuss this particular phenomenon in a later chapter.

---

155   "15% fewer homicides in states with universal background checks," *Futurity News* (retrieved June 9, 2019) https://medium.com/futurity-news/15-fewer-homicides-in-states-with-universal-background-checks-2be0e98d0382

156   To be sure, for nearly a century after the Declaration of Independence, Americans "enjoyed" legalized slavery. People of color were not permitted to have firearms, lest they do the intelligent thing, *i.e.*, turn them on their masters. The Confederacy could probably have used the help in the Civil War, but arming slaves did not seem like a good move. The Union was not so squeamish, and did employ Black units—segregated, of course—and the North ultimately engaged nearly 200,000 black soldiers, of whom around *40,000 died* during the war. Indeed, segregated military units became a mainstay of American forces for nearly another century, until President Harry Truman formally integrated the United States Army in the late 1940s.

Urban and suburban life is not well set up for shooting wildlife for food. One who still wishes to hunt for food must generally pack up their vehicle, and drive several hours to an established rural game region and blow away the wildlife *there*. Further, the local police department will likely arrive within minutes of the 911 call were one to discharge their firearm in a typical urban or suburban area.

To be sure, quite a few American suburbanites may have chosen suburban life to get away from the people of color living nearby in the cities. The isolation of suburban life itself and the extraordinarily high incidents of pharmaceutical intake seem to generate paranoia that *the police may not arrive "in time."* Hence, many suburbanites believe that they need a gun (or two, or more) in the house "to keep safe." Many city dwellers also perceive themselves as living in high-crime areas, and they believe that they, too, need a gun at home. Some of the largest American cities, such as New York, Washington, D.C., or Chicago, for example, do tend to be the most aggressive at trying to enforce gun regulations in the sensible, it turns out, belief that less gun regulation will lead inexorably to more gun violence. Nonetheless, perhaps because of the amazingly outsized influence of the firearms trade association mouthpiece called the "National Rifle Association," gun ownership, or if you like, "firearms homicide on demand," remains extraordinarily popular in huge swaths of the US. This is true even in what are considered some "liberal" suburbs, albeit less so in "liberal" cities, where cheek-to-jowl living will get more people killed in the crossfire. The reason for this is, of course, feudalism.

In the early 21st century, given the insanely high, as it were, incidence of American mental health issues, and the insane lethality of American firearms available for sale to the public, and how many firearms are already "out there," one might believe that at least marginal steps would be taken to "manage" gun violence. One would think that a country where guns account for over 30,000 deaths per year would even make this a priority. One would be terribly, terribly wrong in thinking so. One must consider what agency the typical

American has over most details of his own life. It turns out, of course, that, other than the ability to threaten or kill another human being with a firearm, the typical American has surprisingly little agency over his or her own life. Americans understand that *they have no power politically,* unless and only until they personally invest millions of dollars into campaign contributions and lobbyists, a luxury that only a tiny fraction of people can meaningfully pursue. Americans understand that *they have little to no power in their work place.* After all, American labor practices bear numerous indicia of ostensible slavery such as "employment at will," a legal "minimum wage" close to or below subsistence in most of the country, and no guaranteed legal protections such as mandatory maternity or sick leave or child care or old age pensions or "health insurance" or even vacations.

Even within their own families, Americans are watching their own households implode at a never-before-seen rate. Over 35 million Americans live in single-person households (up from less than 1/3 of that as recently as 1970) and around 40 million Americans live in single-parent-with-children households (about 1/3 of them are the parents themselves, and five out of six of those single parents are women). [157] While the majority of American children are still raised in two-parent households, of these, around just under half involve both parents working full time. [158] These trends are playing out as more men, particularly the less skilled and less educated, seem to just be dropping out of the work force altogether, just as more women are dropping into it. [159] In short, even at home, Americans' agency over their own lives is disappearing. At the same time, political participation and social participation in civic organizations of all kinds is also declining. Total *non*-participation in religious service

---

157   Wolf, Jennifer, "The Single Parent Statistics Based on Census Data," *Very Well Family* (May 22, 2018) https://www.verywellfamily.com/single-parent-census-data-2997668
158   "Raising Kids and Running a Household: How Working Parents Share the Load," *Pew Research Center* (Nov, 4, 2015) https://www.pewsocialtrends.org/2015/11/04/raising-kids-and-running-a-household-how-working-parents-share-the-load/
159   "The Disappearing Male Worker," *Pew Research Center* (Sep. 3, 2013) https://www.pewresearch.org/fact-tank/2013/09/03/the-disappearing-male-worker/

nearly doubled from 13% to 22% from 1990 to 2008, for example. [160] We observe that Barack Obama's much-maligned campaign fundraiser quip that the Americans of the so-called flyover country deal with their ever-more-tenuous situations by "clinging to their religion and guns" [161] was incorrect. Americans are just clinging to *their guns*. One thing we can say about the United States as an industrial power is that American Exceptionalism is truly at its apex in the area of the manufacture and distribution of firearms. So we ask an existential question. In a nation that leads the world in anxiety disorders and in gun ownership, as a vast feeling of powerlessness sinks into an already anxiety-laden and demoralized population as its feudal masters remind the masses of their powerlessness and disposability, what could *possibly* go wrong?

---

160   Briggs, David, "Is Religion in America in Decline?" *HuffPost* (June 2, 2011) https://www.huffpost.com/entry/is-religion-in-america-in_b_843801

161   Pilkington, Ed, "Obama Angers Midwest Voters With Remark About Religion and Guns," *The Guardian* https://www.theguardian.com/world/2008/apr/14/barackobama.uselections2008

12. Jailhouse Rock

YET ANOTHER AREA WHERE the United States is number one in the world is holding prisoners. The US holds something like 2.2 million prisoners [162] in its various federal, state, and local gulag archipelagos at any given moment. [163] Many millions more are under some kind of penal supervision, on parole or probation, house arrest, or the like. China, an actual totalitarian police state with a population four to five times that of the United States, only has about a million-and-a-half prisoners! The American incarceration rate of 700 or so per 100,000 is *also* a world best.

Much has been written about American policies of mass incarceration. One of the main critiques is that the American penal system contains more than a tinge of racial bias in decisions to charge, prosecute, and incarcerate. This should not cause surprise given the undeniable overrepresentation of African-Americans in the prison system. Black people represent around 40% of prisoners despite representing only around 13% of the population. This has led to a situation of more black men held in American penal servitude in the early 21st century than were enslaved in the middle of the 19th century (*see* footnote 48).

This is a bit of an oversimplification. Like much else in the American system, the purpose of the prison industrial complex is to

---

162   "Highest to Lowest – Prison Population Total," *World Prison Brief* (Institute for Prison Policy Research) (retrieved June 9, 2019) http://www.prisonstudies.org/highest-to-lowest/prison-population-total?field_region_taxonomy_tid=All
163   Sawyer, Wendy and Wagner, Peter, "Mass Incarceration: The Whole Pie 2019" *Prison Policy Initiative* (March 19, 2019) https://www.prisonpolicy.org/reports/pie2019.html

advance and maintain the core American value, ostensible *slavery*. I do not necessarily mean the classic, racially based chattel slavery of the 19th century, despite the obvious appearance of *just that* in many of America's prisons. In many American jurisdictions, one can look around many courtrooms and see a disproportionate number of people of color facing criminal charges. Most people in the system will eventually plead guilty to *something* in order to get out of the clutches of a potentially draconian sentence. Unfortunately, by doing so, they will likely permanently stigmatize themselves as "convicted criminals." I suggest that the prison industrial complex is just another social control mechanism to make sure that people understand where they stand in the American system: you are a master, or you are a slave. If you do not *already know* that you are a master, then you are a slave.

One startling reality of the American prison system is that it is far larger than most people think it already is. Another startling reality is that the prison industrial complex is housing *hundreds of thousands of people not convicted* of any crime.

As I write this in 2019, the Trump Administration in the United States is cracking down on all forms of (non-white) immigration, including maintaining vast internment camps near the southern border with Mexico. Indeed, Trump Administration practices include separating small children from their parents, possibly *permanently*, a barbaric as well as illegal policy. The attention that this issue has garnered has focused public attention on the immigrant detention component of the gulag archipelago that *officially* detains around 49,000 people pending asylum hearings or eventual deportation.

Immigration detention, which almost certainly vastly exceeds the 49,000 "official number" as of mid-2019, is just one component of the large number of people held in American carceral institutions who have not been convicted of crimes, although they are, of course, usually guilty of being poor.

Most American states and municipalities have a system of "cash bail." Despite the Eighth Amendment of the Constitution's mandate that "excessive bail ought not to be required," bail that is beyond the reach of many remains a standard operating procedure. Indeed, the bail bond industry has grown up now, complete with its own lobbyists to make sure that excessive bail shall continue to be required in as many jurisdictions as possible. The purpose of bail is to create a strong monetary incentive to show up on a given court date. Anecdotal evidence, however, suggests that jurisdictions that have reduced the use of cash bail often find little or no difference in appearance rates, indeed, even improvements at times. [164] The harsh reality "on the ground" is that in many of the larger American jurisdictions, people *not convicted of crimes* still face time behind bars for no other reason than the inability to come up with cash, or inadequate assets, to get a bail bondsman to do so. To be sure, lengthy pre-trial incarceration is often an excellent incentive to get people to plea bargain, *i.e.,* to confess to some crime whether they committed it or not just to get a definite outcome. Certainty becomes critical in a penal system that threatens draconian sentences for what amount to status crimes associated with being poor, or, especially in federal drug crimes cases, being poor and black. According to a *New York Times* study, a staggering 97% of federal criminal cases and 94% of state criminal cases end in plea bargains, rather than trials. [165]

Once one does enter a plea bargain, their sentence is usually then determined, often resulting in time served and/or probation, rather than further jail time. In terms of the social stigma of having a criminal conviction on one's record, however, the damage is complete. This stigma attaches to everything from eligibility for certain government benefits, to job prospects, to the ability to vote in a number of states. Although American television and popular culture are replete with "the courtroom drama," the reality is that the actual American courtroom typically consists of large groups of

164   *See e.g.,* "Impact of Changes to Pretrial Release Rules," *Maryland Judiciary, 2017* (retrieved June 10, 2019) https://mdcourts.gov/sites/default/files/import/media/newsitem/reference/pdfs/impactofbailreviewreport.pdf
165   Goode, Erica, "Stronger Hand for Judges in the 'Bazaar' of Plea Deals," *The New York Times* (Mar. 22, 2012) https://www.nytimes.com/2012/03/23/us/stronger-hand-for-judges-after-rulings-on-plea-deals.html

relatively poor people waiting for a few moments of attention from a prosecutor and a judge or magistrate. During those few moments, their version of events in that tiny minority of cases not resolved by a plea bargain will be conveyed by a harried, underpaid, and overworked public defender, or perhaps, by a private attorney paid the legal equivalent of the minimum wage to represent "indigent" defendants.

By analogy, what most middle-class people think of as the judicial system is actually a variant of either the business class or first-class section of an airplane. The ordinary middle-class defendant should be able and willing to drain his or her resources in order to pay private counsel to purchase "reasonable doubt for a reasonable fee," or, more likely, a far better plea bargain than would be offered to the "indigent defendant" peasants. The more affluent can buy yet more "boutique treatment" in a system that looks perilously like justice for the highest bidder. [166] In all too many cases, the American justice system creates the impression that it is the best system that money can buy.

This is best illustrated in the ultimate and most somber duty of the American justice system, the imposition of the death penalty. At the death penalty level, and as I write this in 2019, 31 of the 50 states officially have the death penalty on their books, as does the American federal government and military.[167] It is understood that most defendants sentenced to death are relatively poor people who have some form of appointed counsel; indeed, many question the quality of their state-provided representation. [168]

This, in turn, relates to the main event in American mass incarceration, the combination of general leniency for crimes that white defendants are likely to be charged with, and draconian

---

166   This is an even more common appearance in civil cases, where well-financed litigants often crush their opponents under the weight of endless collateral litigation (such as "discovery" and "motion practice") that the American judiciary has permitted litigants to weaponize, apparently for this purpose.
167   Sawe, Benjamin Elisha, "States With The Death Penalty," *World Atlas* (Jan. 16, 2018) https://www.worldatlas.com/articles/states-with-the-death-penalty.html
168   "Death Penalty Representation," *Death Penalty Information Center* (retrieved June 10, 2019) https://deathpenaltyinfo.org/death-penalty-representation

penalties for the crimes that non-white defendants are likely to be charged with. This might explain why there are hundreds of thousands of people incarcerated for various drug-related crimes, especially prevalent in the federal system, where around half of the prison population is there for a drug-related offense. [169] According to at least one study, black men are likely to get around 20% more prison time than a white counterpart *for the same offense* in the federal system. [170] A defining feature of the American criminal justice system is that prosecutors have prosecutorial discretion not to charge at all. This presents a particular problem where prosecutors stand for election, and might receive campaign contributions from donors who might have interests in their prosecuting, or not prosecuting, certain parties. One infamous case involves the daughter and son-in-law of the current President of the US. [171] This broad prosecutorial discretion is also a feature of the federal system and frequently results in seemingly arbitrary outcomes. [172] Prosecutors can add serious prison time for low-level offenders even where the defendant's involvement was minimal *if* the crime happened to include guns or drugs, for example. Seemingly trivial acts, such as *legally buying cold medicines* that somehow end up in the hands of methamphetamine lab operators, could land one a *mandatory minimum* sentence of 5-10 years in prison. [173] Simply put, according to studies, the US has more draconian sentences for most categories of crimes than its peer nations. [174] Of course, a policy that results in holding around one-quarter of the entire world's prisoners

---

169   "Trends in U.S. Corrections," *The Sentencing Project*, (retrieved June 10, 2019) https://www.sentencingproject.org/wp-content/uploads/2016/01/Trends-in-US-Corrections.pdf

170   Lopez, German, "Report: black men get longer sentences for the same federal crime as white men," *Vox* (Nov. 17, 2017) https://www.vox.com/identities/2017/11/17/16668770/us-sentencing-commission-race-booker

171   Bernstein, Andrea, et als., "How Ivanka Trump and Donald Trump, Jr., Avoided a Criminal Indictment," *The New Yorker* (Oct. 4, 2017) https://www.newyorker.com/news/news-desk/how-ivanka-trump-and-donald-trump-jr-avoided-a-criminal-indictment

172   Andersson, Emma, "Why Low-Level Offenders Can Get Longer Sentences Than Airplane Hijackers," *ACLU.org* (May 24, 2018) https://www.aclu.org/blog/smart-justice/sentencing-reform/why-low-level-offenders-can-get-longer-sentences-airplane

173   Stamm, Alex, "The Reality of Federal Drug Sentencing," *ACLU.org* (Nov. 27, 2012) https://www.aclu.org/blog/smart-justice/mass-incarceration/reality-federal-drug-sentencing

174   Fact Sheet: Sentencing, *Justice Policy Institute* (April 2011) http://www.justicepolicy.org/uploads/justicepolicy/documents/sentencing.pdf

is expensive. Aside from the estimated direct costs to federal, state, and local governments of $80 billion per year to operate the nation's prisons, the overall economic cost of this disposition has been estimated to exceed one *trillion* dollars, or around 5% of the American GDP, much of it falling on communities and families of the incarcerated or on the incarcerated themselves. [175]

What a country.

175   Townes, Carimah, "The True Cost of Mass Incarceration Exceeds $1 Trillion," *ThinkProgress* (Sept. 12, 2016) https://thinkprogress.org/the-true-cost-of-mass-incarceration-exceeds-1-trillion-60a6daa69f9d/

13. Life if You Can Call it That in the 'Burbs

AMERICANS CONSUME MORE PETROLEUM than anyone else on Earth. Americans' annual energy consumption is on the order of magnitude of 20% of the world's total energy use with the United States having only about 5% of the planet's population. Up and coming industrial super-power China recently edged out the United States for top spot in total energy consumption at about 20% as well, but China also has about 20% of the world's people. [176]

There are numerous causes for and implications of this relevant to our discussion of American Exceptionalism. For example, although China sells its people more cars and *has* more cars than the United States, American drivers continue to log more miles in their (aging) vehicles. [177] This is the result of decades of deliberate American government policies to disperse people out of cities. [178] Regardless of why the suburbs were set up the way they have been set up, the American suburb is truly the pinnacle, the omega point, if you like, of American Exceptionalism, so important that a legal framework had to be created for it. [179] As of World War II,

---

176   "Countries with highest Primary Energy Consumption," *The Shift Project Data Portal* (retrieved June 10, 2019) http://www.tsp-data-portal.org/TOP-20-consumer#tspQvChart
177   Edelstein, Stephen, "U.S. to Stay Global First in Vehicle Miles Driven, Says Futurist," *Green Car Reports* (Apr. 14, 2014) https://www.greencarreports.com/news/1091470_u-s-to-stay-global-first-in-vehicle-miles-driven-says-futurist
178   Zuegel, Devon, "The Government Created American Suburbia," *Foundation for Economic Education* (Oct. 20, 2017) https://fee.org/articles/the-government-created-american-suburbia/
179   Shill, Gregory H., "Americans shouldn't have to drive, but the law insists on it," *The Atlantic* (July 9, 2019) https://www.theatlantic.com/ideas/archive/2019/07/car-crashes-arent-always-unavoidable/592447/

suburbs, outlying districts of cities, especially residential areas, accounted for perhaps one in eight American residents. Today, that number is around one in two. [180] In the American context, the suburb is the pinnacle of the aphorism that "a man's home is his castle." More to the point, it is a man's *entire medieval manor*. The American suburban home *must* have a bright green lawn, helped to be that way with irrigated water regardless of ground water or precipitation conditions in that part of the country. Heavy use of chemical fertilizers and pesticides is also required. The bright green lawn, of course will remind one of a king in his vast royal estate. Said king now inhabits his castle in the American suburbs. That royal estate must *not* contain anything remotely practical, such as a kitchen garden, or a chicken coop, or even a woodworking shop or tool shed, because if it did, the neighborhood association would unquestionably object to its unsightly nature. Indeed, there is a good chance it might be altogether *illegal*. [181]

Ideally, the suburban estate must have a garage, preferably a two or more car garage. There must be accumulated "storage" of household items in the garage. To be sure, the suburban American must have at least a car, and preferably two or more to qualify for "the middle class." [182] Ideally, at least one car is never to enter the garage.

You will observe that the centerpiece of *all* American "suburban life" is the automobile. Americans have taken "car culture" to its own level of art form. Starting in California with "car hop" restaurants and advancing to "drive-thru windows," car culture is, well, the American culture. For many restaurant outlets, the "drive-thru window" serves more "fast-food meals" than the "eat -in" counter. Americans have taken to eating in their cars to degrees never

---

180   Kolko Jed, "How Suburban Are Big American Cities?" *Five Thirty Eight.com* (May 21, 2015) https://fivethirtyeight.com/features/how-suburban-are-big-american-cities/
181   Leibrock, Amy, "Believe it or not, it may be illegal to grow your own food," *Sustainable America,* (Apr. 30, 2018) https://sustainableamerica.org/blog/believe-it-or-not-it-may-be-illegal-to-grow-your-own-food/
182   Indeed, to properly be in the middle class, there must be adequate off-street parking for the vehicles (even if they are on blocks), though this rule is flexible depending on the region.

imagined. Indeed, as of the early 21ˢᵗ century, it is hard to find a major American intersection without at least two corners, and sometimes three or all four, occupied by a franchised fast-food restaurant with a drive-thru window.

Americans, sadly, are increasingly *sleeping* in their cars, particularly when economic circumstances render the car owner and his or her family homeless, having lost a fixed real estate address. Advances in computers and mobile communications permit Americans to *work* in their cars, as well as talk on the phone and watch television (unfortunately, often *while driving*). Perhaps someone can develop technology to permit full-on bathroom facilities within the ordinary passenger motor vehicle or sport utility vehicle. Then there will never be any need to leave the car *at all.*

The true genius of the American suburb from the standpoint of the only thing that matters in the United States, *profit,* is the total dependency upon a properly functioning automobile. Most Americans would be trapped without access to a car. A popular sounding talking point among American "sustainable planners" is "walkable cities." One observes that until the American suburb came along, "walkable city" simply meant "city." The current prevalence of American vehicles coupled with the deliberate decision of many municipalities to site high-volume traffic roadways through residential areas *without sidewalks or even walkable shoulders* together with long, point-to-point distances means that many locations in the American landscape, especially "the suburbs," are simply not "walkable." Indeed, they are not even "bike-able."

This presents a number of interesting implications. It is a particularly troubling problem from a health standpoint, even if Americans did not already have a slight obesity problem, ranked 12th worst in the world behind some Pacific islands and Kuwait. [183]

A few minor obesity problems aside, as we have observed, one's status as a member of the American middle class does depend on

---

183   Dillinger, Jessica, "The Most Obese Countries in the World," *World Atlas* (last updated Feb. 16, 2018) https://www.worldatlas.com/articles/29-most-obese-countries-in-the-world.html

traveling around in a motor vehicle. Thus, the suburbs are as much a state of mind as they are an actual blight on the physical landscape. To be sure, there was a "white flight" element to the formation of some American suburbs. Racially charged code words such as "better schools" or "open spaces" or "fresh air" were reasons that families would seek out life in the American suburbs. Of course, there were also government policies of subsidized mortgage loans to purchase suburban property, just as inner-city properties were "red-lined" and almost impossible to finance. [184] The central government always provided funding for road and infrastructure construction for the suburbs, funding usually not made available to aging inner cities.

One aspect of life that suburban exiles were running *away from* in the urban centers was public transportation. After all, why go through all the trouble of fleeing to cultural wastelands and incur a lengthy daily commute to get away from "those people" if you are just going to bump into them again on a crowded train or bus? Hence, many suburbs are "underserved" by public transit, if they are served at all. Indeed, in many suburbs, the only form of public transit is the uniquely American concept of the yellow school bus that takes schoolchildren to and from school exactly once per day each way. Many younger people are starting to find that the suburbs are a cultural and environmental wasteland. Faced with the high cost of living there caused by increasing rising property taxes and the expenses of owning multiple motor vehicles and the logistical difficulties of having two parents having to work far away from home with small children, many younger people have started to return to city centers. This has been particularly true in the large coastal cities with booming job markets, especially New York and San Francisco.

Still, many older people, *especially* white people, prefer the "my home is my armed fortress" style of living that only the American suburbs can offer. The overall geography of the suburbs remains *disorienting*. One author has described the suburban layout as "the

---

184   Zuegel, Devon Marisa, "How We Subsidize Suburbia," *The American Conservative* (Oct. 20, 2017) https://www.theamericanconservative.com/urbs/we-have-always-subsidized-suburbia/

geography of nowhere." [185] Lengthy roads and highways lead in turn to endlessly un-differentiated residential subdivisions consisting entirely of similar-looking, detached, single-family homes with front and back yards. There are often streets featuring cul-de-sacs. Found amidst these "features" is the occasional shopping center usually located at large interchanges and perhaps a school or a pocket park. The suburbs, for the most part, do not sport agricultural activity. Woodlands or wetlands of any note are uncommon, and usually there is little or no discernible industrial or commercial activity except, of course, in office parks or the even more oxymoronic term "industrial park." If there is public transit at all, stops on the few available bus routes are often quite a long walk from many homes. Established train or trolley routes as one would expect virtually anywhere in Europe and in much of Asia and even in parts of Africa and Latin America are unusual in the American suburb. The American suburb also has a number of other ingenious features. Life in the 'burbs can be psychologically devastating, as the suburbs physically enforce aloneness and isolation from other human beings. As Americans get older and their children move away and their spouses die or they get divorced, more and more Americans find themselves in single-occupant households. Indeed, single-occupancy households now stand at a record 28% of all American households. [186]

The American suburbs are also wonderfully toxic on several other levels. One can rarely just walk outside and see other people; one must *drive* somewhere. This has proven very useful for the profit of the pharmaceutical and health care industries, particularly to treat lifestyle diseases like diabetes and attendant obesity, and, of course, depression and anxiety disorders.

The suburban lifestyle strongly encourages envy of one's neighbors. Their homes and any expensive toys such as motor

---

185   Kuntsler, James Howard, *The Geography of Nowhere* (Simon & Schuster: 1994) https://kunstler.com/books/the-geography-of-nowhere/
186   Joyner, James, "Record 28% of American Households One Person Only," *Outside the Beltway.com* (Feb. 1, 2012) https://www.outsidethebeltway.com/record-28-of-american-households-one-person-only/

vehicles—sports cars or SUVs or motor homes—or boats and the like are clearly visible. To be sure, social media has also done wonders in this department, encouraging its clients to pitch their own happy lives, complete with pictures in a way designed to make those viewing feel both jealous and inadequate, all in an effort to try to assuage *their own* sense of personal inadequacy!

The suburban lifestyle is also fabulous for requiring as much non-renewable energy to be used as excessively as possible. Of course, one needs to own multiple motor vehicles. The necessarily bright green lawn will require chemical fertilizer and insecticide, and water even amidst droughts. The split-level, ranch, colonial, hacienda, or other form of McMansion house will require a plethora of utility connections to operate. These will be necessary to heat and cool the house, as well as to bring in water, and to light it and run the kitchen, just as it already required a plethora of inputs to build it and clear the land it is on in the first place. Because of this, virtually all American policies are devoted to artificially suppressing the price of energy (especially of motor fuels), and encouraging waste; we discuss this further in a later chapter. As an added bonus, many suburbs, like many urban areas, have even become "food deserts." These areas have few, if any, supermarkets or outlets to buy fresh food for preparation or consumption, but still plenty of fast-food outlets. Amazingly, although unlike apartment dwellers, suburban dwellers usually have the space and sunlight for at least a small kitchen garden, less than 1/3 of American households grow any amount of food at all for themselves. [187] Indeed, the separation from nature, other people, and for that matter, *reality* ("alienation") is pretty much the default condition of "living" in the American suburbs. Alienation is a term from Marxist economic and social theory representing a forced separation, by the forces of capitalism, of people from things and other people to which they should feel attachment. Marxist theory of alienation usually

---

187   Kongs, Jennifer, "US Households Grow Home Food Gardens," *Mother Earth News* (Oct. 8, 2010) https://www.motherearthnews.com/organic-gardening/home-food-gardens-zb0z10zkon

concerns itself with issues of labor and production. [188] Thus, a worker engaged in production is then "alienated" from his ultimate product. In the American suburbs, people are also "alienated" from their own human nature. The American suburb, which came into being in its present form several decades after Marx's death, really does represent a wonderful pinnacle of alienation.

To be sure, workers in the service economy or in management who deal with nothing but paper, or, as is much more likely these days, bouncing electronic images on computer screens are alienated from the production of things. Compare, if you will, the life of a medieval guild member who made, say, a cooking implement or a piece of furniture, or a peasant who grew vegetables or herded livestock. They would not be alienated from the products of their labor. It is quite possible that the average office worker will never so much as see or touch the product or, for that matter, be able to coherently describe what it is.

Although we have discussed the severe inequalities in American income and wealth distribution, that is not the particular point of our discussion of the American suburbs. The suburbs often house the winners of capitalism, the upper-middle class of management and even the ownership class. We observe that even *the winners* of American capitalism often find themselves alienated in these conditions, because life in the suburbs fundamentally alienates people from reality, even for the affluent.

We continue our look at life in the suburbs with birth. In so-called primitive or indigenous communities, childbirth (including maternal care) falls into the province of the extended family, usually the female members of the extended family. The specifics of birth itself *might* involve a specialist, perhaps with the title midwife, still in use even in so-called advanced countries. Or it might just involve (female) family members. In the United States, childbirth is in the hands of credentialed specialists with advanced medical degrees.

---

188   "Marxist Theory of Alienation," *Communication Theory* (retrieved June 12, 2019) https://www.communicationtheory.org/marxist-theory-of-alienation/

Ideally, they will manage the birth process in the most clinical and profit-driven way possible, although, hospitals for the upper-middle class do often feature birthing rooms and the like these days. Modern medicine has brought about numerous miracles; indeed, it has probably saved my own life on a number of occasions. As such, it would be good if the US could do better than *dead last* among developed countries in measures of maternal health, or in many measures of children's health. [189] Assuming that mom and child both survived childbirth and made their way home, in order to afford suburban living, it is likely that both parents will have to remain in the work force. We already know that the United States is uniquely bad in this department by failing to provide for *any* mandatory paid maternity leave time to have the child, let alone paid maternal leave for the initial stages of child rearing. Hence, arranging child care will become a necessity.

For virtually every society on Earth until the mid-20th century, the default child care provider was the extended family. Most families lived and worked together, usually doing some kind of farm work, or possibly some kind of artisanal work or, perhaps both. Usually, the family unit would include grandparents, aunts, uncles, and cousins, as well as the usual nuclear parents with children arrangement. The extended family lived in the same dwelling, or at least very close by. This arrangement easily permitted child care within the family defined as broadly as necessary.

The initial stages of industrial capitalism did not necessarily change this dispensation. Even if both parents and at a certain age, the children themselves worked outside of the home in industrial activities, members of the extended family were often still available.

As the 20th century evolved, however, particularly in the period after the Second World War which coincided with the rise of the American suburbs, the suburban starter home typically did not afford enough room for an extended family. Furthermore, the

---

189   Dockterman, Eliana, "U.S. Ranks Worst Developed Country for Maternal Health," *Time* (May 6, 2015) http://time.com/3847755/mothers-children-health-save-the-children-report/

US was entering a unique and temporary period where a single breadwinner's activity in the work place could support an entire nuclear family in a suburban home. That same salary could also support the acquisition of at least two motor vehicles; these, in turn, could easily transport the nuclear family, let us call them George, his wife Jane, daughter Judy, and his boy Elroy, to a weekly dinner with the in-laws, which could be back in the city or in another suburb.

Most importantly to the dispensation, Jane (mommy) did not have to work. Of course, quite a few women *did* work, often in the education field or nursing or other so-called women's professions.

For those cases of the single (male) breadwinner, mommy staying home allowed the traditional default child-rearing arrangement, bringing up a child by members of his or her own family. For the most part, professional women who worked outside of the home earned more than enough, especially when the wife's wages were added to husband's pay, to afford professional child care. US-government statistics suggest that the percentage of women in the work force was around 30% in 1950, and that increased to about 47% in 2000. [190] At the same time, women's labor force participation rate grew from 34% in 1950 to 60% in 2000; this was more or less unchanged by 2010. [191]

As 20th century suburban life rolled on, economics dictated that two working parents were essential to maintaining a middle-class lifestyle for millions of families. Under these circumstances, *both children and their parents* became alienated from their traditional filial relationships, as an unrelated *paid intermediary* became necessary to support the basic middle-class lifestyle. Besides child care, the American suburbs also required the growth of other professional intermediaries. These included gardeners and landscapers tending to the all-important bright green, chemically fertilized lawns and ornamental shrubs framing the lawn and

190   Toosi, Mitra, "A century of change: the U.S. labor force 1950-2020," *Monthly Labor Review* (May 2002) https://www.bls.gov/opub/mlr/2002/05/art2full.pdf
191   "Women in the Labor Force," *U.S. Dept. of Labor, Women's Bureau, Publications* (retrieved June 9, 2019) https://www.dol.gov/wb/factsheets/qf-laborforce-10.htm

the *manse*, pool maintainers, house cleaners, and an entire class of food-service professionals cooking outside the home. Of course, suburban life also requires an entire array of service providers just for the motor vehicle, from fueling and maintenance and repair, to washing and detailing. All of this alienation of suburbanites from their loved ones, their environment, and their lives takes place as the background noise of the suburbs. We have not even gotten to work yet in order to observe the classic Marxist alienation from production!

Just to remind you, suburbanites tend to be *the winners* in American capitalism. Let us not give another thought to the alienation suffered by *the losers*.

14. POVERTY OF SPIRIT

AS A GENERAL PLATITUDE, it is understood that the United States is the richest country on Earth and almost certainly the richest country in the history of humanity. Wealth distribution, however, is wildly unequal. Thus, the United States ranks an abysmal 36th or 37th out of 41 developed countries on most measures of child poverty. [192] In your face, Chile, Bulgaria, Romania, and Mexico!

At the same moment that the United States is unable to provide *food security* for around one in five American children and American workers face a paycheck-to-paycheck lifestyle at the rate of four in five, according to a recent survey, [193] the US is home to around 600 of the world's 1,800 billionaires. [194] American wealth inequality is so extreme that three individuals (Warren Buffett, Jeff Bezos, and Bill Gates) have more wealth than 50% of the American population, *i.e.*, over 160 million people. [195] Given all of this, then, it seems almost inevitable that the US would rank in the worst position in terms

192   Edmond, Charlotte, "These rich countries have high levels of child poverty," *World Economic Forum* (June 28, 2017) https://www.weforum.org/agenda/2017/06/these-rich-countries-have-high-levels-of-child-poverty/
193   Martin, Emmie, "The government shutdown spotlights a bigger issue: 78% of US workers live paycheck to paycheck," *CNBC* (Jan. 10, 2019) https://www.cnbc.com/2019/01/09/shutdown-highlights-that-4-in-5-us-workers-live-paycheck-to-paycheck.html
194   Chenel, Thomas and Moynihan, Ruqayyah, "These are the 19 countries with the most billionaires in the world," *Business Insider France* (Dec. 27, 2018) https://www.businessinsider.com/these-are-the-19-countries-with-the-most-billionaires-in-the-world-2018-10
195   Kirsch, Noah, "The 3 Richest Americans Hold More Wealth Than Bottom 50% Of The Country, Study Finds," *Forbes* (Nov. 9, 2017) https://www.forbes.com/sites/noahkirsch/2017/11/09/the-3-richest-americans-hold-more-wealth-than-bottom-50-of-country-study-finds/

of the overall poverty rate among the world's 35 leading developed countries. [196]

Fortunately, we can always count on the American right-wing to justify the current insanely unequal disposition [197] regardless of how patently unjust or, if you prefer, insane this might be. Thus, apologists for American capitalism insist that as long as American poor people live better than poor people in sub-Saharan Africa or medieval peasants, who it should be noted, had far more leisure time than the average American worker, there is simply nothing to complain about.[198] In short, it is just plain *unfair* to call such people poor even as we add housing insecurity and overall economic insecurity to the food insecurity we have already discussed. [199]

Nonetheless, despite these grim realities, for most Americans, corporate welfare and tax holidays for the super-rich remain politically viable in the United States. On the other hand, anything that might improve the lives of the poor, especially the working poor, will draw the charge of the most reviled world in the American vocabulary: socialism. Needless to say, centuries of proper conditioning have convinced most poor Americans (at least the whites) that as long as there is someone else that they can look down upon (that would be the non-whites), then they are a mere lottery ticket away from joining the rich themselves. If they have not made it or even if they *never* make it, it *certainly* has nothing to do with the structural realities of late-stage capitalism and *must be* because they or their children just aren't good enough or haven't worked hard enough.

Hence, they will continue to vote against any politician who suggests any measure of socialism, even amidst their own economic insecurity.

America, what a country.

196   Fay, Bill, "Poverty in the United States," *Debt.org* (retrieved June 12, 2019) https://www.debt.org/faqs/americans-in-debt/poverty-united-states/

197   Sheffield, Rachel and Rector, Robert, "Understanding Poverty in the United States: Surprising Facts About America's Poor" *Heritage.org* (Sept. 13, 2011) https://www.heritage.org/poverty-and-inequality/report/understanding-poverty-the-united-states-surprising-facts-about

198   Parramore, Lynn, "The average American worker takes less vacation time than a medieval peasant," *Business Insider* (Nov. 7, 2016) https://www.businessinsider.com/american-worker-less-vacation-medieval-peasant-2016-11

199   Desmond, Matthew and Gershenson, Carl, "Housing and Employment Insecurity Among the Working Poor," *Society for the Study of Social Problems* (Jan. 11, 2016) http://scholar.harvard.edu/files/mdesmond/files/desmondgershenson.sp2016.pdf?m=1452638824

15. FAITH-BASED INITIATIVES

AMERICANS HAVE ALWAYS BEEN big on faith. Freedom of religion is formally enshrined within the First Amendment of the United States Constitution. Common lore taught to American schoolchildren is that Protestant extremists at odds with the Church of England amusingly called "Pilgrims" took their belt buckles and put them on their hats and brought their miserable existences across the Atlantic to the Plymouth colony in what would eventually become Massachusetts. There, they could freely engage in their austere religious practice. Freedom of religious practice was also, at least in part, the basis for the founding of other colonies, including a Catholic colony in Maryland, a Quaker colony in Pennsylvania, and a money-based Dutch colony in New York (the true American religion!). Thus, to this day, religion is a serious issue in US. For the last few decades, many political issues motivated by religious beliefs have dominated "the culture wars." Particularly starting in the 1990s, Wall Street and the Democratic Party conspired to use "culture war" and "wedge issues" such as abortion, [200] gay marriage, and gun control, which could fit the category as to

---

200   Naturally, it is convenient for the powerful to pitch something like abortion as an isolated issue about "fetal life," and of course, a matter of *religious* conscience. Evidently, conscience has nothing to do with the actual welfare of children. Were this the case, Americans might start having to consider broader issues, including prenatal care, the lack of mandatory paid maternity leave and child care, woefully inadequate nutrition and food security for millions of children, inadequate housing, health care, and numerous needs of life that are not presently being provided. Religious zealots holding signs with pictures of fetuses and getting in the face of fraught women trying to get an abortion just do not feel the need to bother thinking about any of this. The American abortion fight carries on in the way it does because it has proven to be effective politics.

many Americans owning guns is a religion, to replace *actual* issues concerning the unfairness and cruelty of the American economic system. As I write this in 2019, both abortion rights and gay marriage currently remain, tenuously, the law of the land. Unfortunately, legalized abortion and same-sex marriage both resulted from contested Supreme Court decisions, and a simple personnel change on the High Court could change this dramatically. The Republican Party has managed to hold control of that Court, and indeed, move it further to the right, through a combination of extreme legislative hardball and by managing to win the 2016 presidential election. I digress. We return now to matters of faith. A recent poll showed that something like 89% of Americans believe in God. [201] This presumably means that 10 or 11% believe in the *non-existence* of God, but who can tell? That same poll showed that 72% believe in angels and 71% believe in Heaven (I guess, 1% believe in a Heaven without angels), and 64% believe in Hell and 61% believe in the Devil (I guess, 3% believe in Hell without the Devil). Another survey puts Americans' belief in aliens, *i.e.,* that aliens from other planets have visited Earth, at around 62%; the same survey puts Americans' belief in ghosts at about 50%. [202] Yet another survey shows that 36% of Americans believe in UFOs—unidentified flying objects—and 10% *believe that they have seen one.* [203]

Indeed, Americans have so many colorful beliefs, that a cursory search of the Internet is sure to turn up gems. One "survey" shows that 35% of Americans believe that gay people can just choose to be straight any time they want. The same survey establishes that 30% of Americans do not know the year of the September 11th attacks. Some 30% of Americans say they believe that the Bible is the literal word of God, 33% deny that they are the product of evolution,

201   Newport, Frank, "Most Americans Still Believe in God," *Gallup,* (June 29, 2016) https://news.gallup.com/poll/193271/americans-believe-god.aspx
202   Smith, Sam Benson, "You'd Be Shocked By How Many Americans Believe in Aliens," *Readers Digest* (retrieved June 10, 2019) https://www.rd.com/culture/number-americans-believe-aliens/
203   Harish, Alon, "UFOs Exist, Say 36% In National Geographic Survey," *ABC News* (June 27, 2012) https://abcnews.go.com/Technology/ufos-exist-americans-national-geographic-survey/story?id=16661311

29% believe that it is high time for an armed revolution against the United States government; and another 29% couldn't find the Pacific Ocean—which takes up nearly half the Earth's surface—on a map. [204] You, Dear Reader, understand that all of this is by design. The egregious practices of American capitalism, *i.e.*, ostensible slavery by another name, would be unacceptable in any country as allegedly prosperous as the United States if something else were not going on. What is going on is not *merely* a dumbed-down media operating in concert with a watered-down education system. What is going on is an intentional divide and conquer strategy that exacerbates the already considerable divisions that are inevitable in a vast and diverse nation of hundreds of millions of people. Indeed, that diversity already consists of both immigrants and descendants of immigrants from all over Europe, Africa, Asia, and Latin America. Nonetheless, the US still maintains itself as culturally English.

The United States has no *official* state religion: the First Amendment to the Constitution states "Congress shall make no law respecting an establishment of religion, or prohibiting the free exercise thereof." Nonetheless, Protestantism still represents about 50% of the religious identities of Americans. As around 20% self-identify as Catholic, this means at least 70% of Americans self-identify as some form of "Christian." [205]

Aside from its religious implications, this culturally English (or Anglo) national identity proves useful for the divide and conquer project. The English managed to conquer much of the world. To be sure, the English simultaneously perfected certain technological advantages, particularly in marine navigation, as well as the application of violence. The skill of the English in employing ethnic divide and conquer tactics in the English colonies even when occupied by densely populated indigenous peoples enabled the English to conquer vast parts of the globe. Whether in Asia, Africa,

---

204   Klee, Miles, "The 11 Dumbest Thing That 30% of Americans Believe," *Daily Dot* (Feb. 25, 2017) https://www.dailydot.com/via/dumb-things-30-percent-america-believes/
205   "Religious Landscape Study," *Pew Research Center* (retrieved June 22, 2019) https://www.pewforum.org/religious-landscape-study/

or the Americas, this combination of skills enabled a nation of just a few million people to acquire an empire of hundreds of millions, and at its peak in the early part of the 20th century, the British Empire held sway over a quarter of the world's land mass and a quarter of the world's people. [206]

The significance to our discussion of American Exceptionalism is that the very same technology employed to pit local indigenous populations against each other in Africa or in India (or even in Ireland) was used just as effectively in North America. There, a wedge first driven between white indentured servants and black indentured servants and Native Americans in North America in the 17th century remains in place. To be sure, a key part of the mythology is that the white English were superior to all others, perhaps the original American faith-based initiative! By the time the English were done with their colonies, colonized peoples were also colonized *in spirit* as well as politically and economically. To this day, there are major industries in the so-called Third World to lighten one's skin to, of course, look more English (to wit, white). [207]

This colonization of spirit is a core defining principle of American Exceptionalism. The victims of a rapacious, one-way feudal system often buy into conceptions of their own inferiority with respect to their betters, *i.e.*, the oligarchs. In the finest English divide and conquer tradition, to this day, Americans cannot seem to form class consciousness across racial lines, thus assuring this result.

One can readily see the results of divide and conquer in American inner cities. In the American inner cities, the education system and criminal justice systems, among others, do what they can to instill absolute hopelessness, particularly in the young. The youth are often steered to a path that leads to crime and their inevitable shunting into the prison industrial complex.

---

206   "When was the peak of the British Empire? What was going on then? What combination of events caused it to start fading?" *Quora.com* (retrieved June 10, 2019) https://www.quora.com/When-was-the-peak-of-the-British-Empire-What-was-going-on-then-What-combination-of-events-caused-it-to-start-fading.

207   *See, e.g.* Rehman, Maliha, "Getting rich from the skin lightening trade," *Business of Fashion* (Sept. 27. 2017) https://www.businessoffashion.com/articles/global-currents/profiting-from-the-skin-lightening-trade

It is not *just* the poor and people of color who buy into their own inferiority. It seems that virtually all Americans who were not "to the manor born" accept this, at least, some of the time. Ordinary Americans are taught that their betters in athletics or academia, or ultimately in business, are superior to them because they have more talent, work harder, deserve it, or simply possess some magic attribute that the typical American never will. Against such *uber-menschen*, one should just not bother even trying to keep up. American Exceptionalism does not permit one to consider the possibility that such people were simply born with more money, and hence superior opportunity. With the American ostensible slave-based system safely embedded in the brains of most American children and adults *as a matter of faith*, we turn to one of the greatest whoppers of them all: American social mobility.

What a country.

16. SOCIAL IMMOBILITY

THE AMERICAN DREAM IS defined at least by at least one online dictionary as "the ideals of freedom, equality and opportunity traditionally held to be available to every American, or a life of personal happiness and comfort as traditionally sought by individuals in the United States." [208] The late, great comedian, George Carlin, quipped, "That's why they call it the American Dream, because you have to be asleep to believe it."

If you have been paying attention to our discussion so far, you recognize that Carlin was on to something. Unless you are rich in the United States, or, at least, well off, which I would arbitrarily define as a net worth in excess of $10 million per person, you are simply not going anywhere in the American hierarchy. Neither are your children. The traditional *driver* of the American Dream is the concept of social mobility. Social mobility is the ability of individuals or groups to move upward (or downward) in status based on wealth, occupation, education, or some other social variable. Put another way, if I only work hard enough, I can have a better life for my family, especially for my children. The American mythos is that people from all over the globe seek to better their lives by coming to America, where their ambitions and hard work will enable them to get unimaginably better lives than they could have back home. Of course, compared to other countries, such as the high-tax/high-regulation European

---

208   "American Dream," *Dictionary.com* (retrieved June 10, 2019) https://www.dictionary.com/browse/american-dream

economies that American capitalism is supposedly so superior to, things do not look so good for social mobility. By the measure of how well sons perform economically compared to their fathers, at least one survey has the US coming in 14th out of 18 countries studied in this area of social mobility. [209] Indeed, other studies show an overall decline in American lifetime earnings mobility. [210] The conclusion from the data is that in the early 21st century, it is unlikely that an American worker will advance much, at least on the income hierarchy, from the position where they find themselves *at age 20*, regardless of their hard work. [211] Thus, the members of the existing American middle class, or at least what is left of it, desperately try to lock down their own privileges and preserve what they can for their children. Among other things, they prefer funding local school districts out of local property taxes, thus guaranteeing that affluent neighborhoods with higher property values will pay more for their public schools. Nearby communities in the same state, or county, *or city*, if they have a lower tax base, will have less tax revenue for schools. Of course, it is not just educational opportunities, but the social capital of the parents' personal and business contacts and the ability to provide funding for homes and cars, and other like factors will play their role in locking in advantages (or disadvantages) of the relevant social stratum. Ominously, for people of color, especially for black Americans, there is indeed some social mobility: middle-class blacks seem to be downwardly mobile. [212] To be sure, there are valid critiques of social mobility analysis, if for no other reason because it expresses things only in relative terms. In absolute terms, however, we might ask just what is happening when something like 78% of

209   Gould, Elise, U.S. lags behind peer countries in mobility," *Economic Policy Institute* (Oct. 10, 2012) https://www.epi.org/publication/usa-lags-peer-countries-mobility/
210   Carr, Michael D. and Weimers, Emily E., "The decline in lifetime earnings mobility in the U.S.: Evidence from survey-linked administrative data," *Washington Center for Equitable Growth* (Sept. 7, 2016) https://equitablegrowth.org/working-papers/the-decline-in-lifetime-earnings-mobility-in-the-u-s-evidence-from-survey-linked-administrative-data/
211   Semuels, Alana, "Poor at 20, Poor for Life," *The Atlantic* (July 14, 2016) https://www.theatlantic.com/business/archive/2016/07/social-mobility-america/491240/
212   Rodrigue, Edward and Reeves, Richard V., "Five Bleak Facts on Black Opportunity," *Brookings* (Jan. 15, 2015) https://www.brookings.edu/blog/social-mobility-memos/2015/01/15/five-bleak-facts-on-black-opportunity/

American full-time workers claim they live paycheck to paycheck as of the beginning of 2019, when only around 40% claimed to be living paycheck to paycheck as recently as 2007, just before the Great Recession started. [213]

This provides ample support for the proposition that American social mobility is dead, both as a relative matter and as an absolute matter. Of course, the rich continue to get richer. [214] Famously, *three people* at the top have more wealth than 160 million people in the lower half of American wealth distribution. It is good to be the king. In American terms, it is not so good to be just about anyone else. Of course, we have the Anglo/American tradition of the "have nots" themselves believing that they are the "have nots" *because they deserve it.* Just as the rich believe they deserve their riches; they especially do not like to acknowledge how much of their 'success' is simply good luck. [215] As John Steinbeck quipped about the American poor, they do not see themselves as an exploited proletariat or peasantry, but simply as "temporarily embarrassed millionaires." While that quip is from nearly a century ago, it seems that ethos is just as strong today among many American poor people. Given the locked-in placements in American income and wealth strata, exacerbated since the Great Recession, temporarily could just mean "quite a while."

213   Pisani, Joseph, "More Upper-Income Workers Living Paycheck to Paycheck," *CNBC* (Aug. 2, 2010) https://www.cnbc.com/id/32862851/
214   Prins, Nomi, "The Rich Are Still Getting Richer," *The Nation* (Feb. 26, 2019) https://www.thenation.com/article/inequality-wealth-rich-still-getting-richer/
215   Dorling, Danny, "Getting rich is largely about luck – shame the wealthy don't want to hear it," *The Conversation* (May 3, 2017), http://theconversation.com/getting-rich-is-largely-about-luck-shame-the-wealthy-dont-want-to-hear-it-77111

17. YOU ARE WHAT YOU EAT

T HE UNITED STATES IS blessed with vast quantities of fresh water and arable land, at least for now. As a result, the United States scores tops in affordability of food among 125 nations surveyed by Oxfam. The United States ends up sixth from the bottom in terms of its unhealthy eating habits, despite its high affordability ranking, and despite coming in fourth in food quality based on availability of nutritionally diverse food options and access to safe water, because of its high diabetes and obesity rates. Thus, despite its overall wealth and food affordability, the US comes in tied for 21st in this ranking of the world's food systems. [216] As we have already discussed, the United States has gone from a largely agrarian country to a country where only a small fraction of its work force is engaged in food production. Nonetheless, the US is an export powerhouse in a number of agriculture commodities, particularly wheat and soybeans, and corn (maize), both for human and animal consumption. To generate such output with a relative minimum of labor input, the American agriculture sector is capital-intensive. It is this capital-intensive and energy-intensive element that will lead our discussion of American Exceptionalism in this category. [217] Unlike virtually every other country on Earth, in the

---

216   Andrews, James, "U.S. Places 21ˢᵗ in Ranking of World Food Systems," *Food Safety News* (Jan. 15, 2014) https://www.foodsafetynews.com/2014/01/u-s-places-21st-in-ranking-of-world-food-systems

217   Canning, Patrick, et als., "Energy Use In the U.S. Food System," *U.S. Dept. of Agriculture Economic Research Report No. 94* (March 2010) http://web.mit.edu/dusp/dusp_extension_unsec/reports/polenske_ag_energy.pdf

US the purpose of growing, processing, distributing, and ultimately cooking, serving, and consuming food is *not the nourishing of people*. Rather, its purpose is the *maximum return on capital* for the benefit of oligarchs. You know this because that is the purpose of *everything* in the US.

We observe that in a country that has an obesity problem, the US uses only about 2% of its farmland to grow fruits and vegetables. [218] Indeed, only around one in ten adult Americans even get enough fruits and vegetables in their diets. [219] Once again, this is because the purpose of agriculture in the US is to grow *money*, not to nourish *people*. Hence, the US devotes nearly 60% of its farmland for the big commodity crops, *e.g.*, wheat, soybeans, corn/maize, and potatoes, and grows them using a heavy chemical, energy, and capital input system.

Perhaps all we need to know is that the US spends substantially more money on its so-called health care than it does on its food. American food is quite inexpensive by world standards for a variety of reasons, but among them is because the US produces so much food mechanically. One can think metaphorically of microwave-safe dishes and ask whether the *food* is actually safe, even if the dish is, or better yet, if the microwaved food is safe for the person *eating* the food. I say this because microwaving food is an excellent paradigm for the American food-delivery system. Energy generated from some distant place (imported oil, far off hydropower, nuclear power, gas, or coal) is used to generate nitrogen fertilizer and pesticides out of chemical inputs, and then, in turn, to operate farming equipment (tractors, irrigation pumps, threshers, etc.). Some labor is involved in operating the capital-intensive equipment, to be sure, but for the bulk of American agricultural products, mostly the major grains,

---

218   "Less Corn, More Fruits and Vegetables Would Benefit U.S. Farmers, Consumers and Rural Communities," *Union of Concerned Scientists* (Oct. 23, 2013) https://www.ucsusa.org/news/press_release/less-corn-more-fruits-and-vegetables-0378.html
219   "Only 1 in 10 Adults Get Enough Fruits or Vegetables," *Centers for Disease Control and Prevention* (Nov. 16, 2017) https://www.cdc.gov/media/releases/2017/p1116-fruit-vegetable-consumption.html

which, in turn, are also often fed to livestock, this often falls into the realm of operating heavy equipment. [220]

Once a crop has matured, a farmer uses specialized machinery for harvesting. Assuming the crop is not processed on site after harvesting, the crop is transported by diesel-powered truck or rail to processing facilities. There, another energy-intensive process converts the raw crop into something more commercially viable for further processing into ready-to-eat foods. The crop may be converted into animal feed or ethanol. An energy intensive process is used to "stretch" gasoline, not because it makes sense from an energy efficiency efficient standpoint, but because it makes sense from the standpoint of political benefit to senators from the American Midwest.

In some parts of the country, farmers grow large swaths of cash crops via irrigation from ancient aquifers or from lakes and rivers that are themselves rapidly depleting. Such crops are often grown entirely for export contrary to any environmental rationality; alfalfa grown in deserts in California and Arizona comes to mind.

Assuming that the crops *used for human food* maintain any nutritional integrity between mechanical harvesting and transport to processing facilities, further processing will likely render the crops into something that can survive still further processing into something generally thought of as food. This might include flour or other inputs of bread, cakes, or crackers, or perhaps corn syrup, which will then become an input into *virtually everything*.

Shelf life is a major concern, as any remaining nutritional elements of the crop are processed so that rodents, insects, bacteria, and the like will leave it alone long enough for an American consumer to buy it. The consumer will likely find the product on a shelf in one of the inner aisles of an American supermarket. The effectiveness of all of this processing explains, for example, how a Hostess Twinkie may survive for centuries if not eaten.

---

220   We will try to confine our discussion to plant-based food materials, because discussing the raising and slaughter of livestock, particularly in the factory farm context, will be even more depressing than the remainder of this work already is.

Assuming that our crop is transformed into flour, or meal, or another typical "input," for reasons of marketing, "vitamin fortification" is chemically added, as are artificial flavors and colors. This will ensure that the ultimate product has the aesthetics (appearance, taste, smell, perhaps texture) of actual food, while in actuality being nothing but a chemical simulacrum of food. [221] The finished food product is then put into brightly colored packaging, and then placed on another diesel-powered conveyance to a food distribution warehouse. From there, the "food" will finally be shipped to a grocery store of some kind or perhaps directly to a consumer's home address via Amazon or another delivery company, and then, finally, the "food" will arrive in a consumer's kitchen.

Obviously, this path applies to the home-consumption model; Americans eat around a third of their meals away from home, representing an even higher percentage in terms of food dollars. [222] Indeed, at the "late processing" stage, there is a category of entirely prepared meals simply brought home and eaten there. This makes sense in a nation where Americans eat the majority of their meals *alone.* [223]

Food is an area of American life where the rubber of alienation in the Marxist sense and in every other sense meets the road in the context of American eating practices. Americans tend to think of issues arising from their food practices the way they view everything else and the same way they live: in isolation. Hence, most policymakers and activists consider such integrally related issues, such as obesity or diabetes (or both, now termed *diabesity*), food deserts or the lack of quality food, *e.g.,* fresh fruits and vegetables, in the diet as entirely discreet and independent problems. Such disparate issues certainly

---

221   Not to worry: the human body will quickly recognize the "food" as something that it cannot digest, quite possibly making "the consumer" ill in the process, likely further adding to the profit of the health care system.

222   Cohen, Nevin, "USDA Charts the Growth of 'Food Away from Home,'" *Urban Food Policy* (July 8, 2016) https://urbanfoodpolicy.com/2016/07/08/usda-charts-the-growth-of-food-away-from-home/

223   Hume, Scott, "Table for One? More than half of meals eaten alone, study finds," *CS Monitor* (Aug. 25, 2014) https://www.csmonitor.com/Business/The-Bite/2014/0825/Table-for-one-More-than-half-of-meals-eaten-alone-study-finds

cannot possibly be symptoms of a vast American existential treadmill which, in the name of profit and power, has been designed to render human beings insane and hence, beyond any ability to threaten the rich and powerful.

One *could* envision hunter-gatherer tribes or bands duly engaged in their hunting and food gathering, preparation, and then communal eating, all while nourishing not just their bodies but their social order, as well. To do so, we need not travel back millennia. We need only think of current First World countries; Italy, France, and Japan come to mind. In such places, much, if not most, food is grown or raised a relatively short distance from where it is prepared for consumption and eaten. The people eating the food have a significant role in either growing the food, or at least in its preparation, serving, and consumption. Such current elite fads as artisanal foods and eating local are, of course, the norm, in places with healthier populations than the US. Sadly, the very common French or Spanish practice of slow eating, long, multi-course meals consisting of small portions dispensed over hours, while sitting and talking with friends and family, is almost unheard of at this point in the fast-food dominated United States. It is unsurprising that the US has also seen a precipitous decline of meals eaten together as a family. [224]

American food and eating practices would seem to be just part of a suite of issues designed to destroy the spirit of individuals. This destruction serves the only two things that matter in the American system: maintenance of profit, and maintenance of power. Americans' abysmal fast-food eating habits even where many who partake of this particular lifestyle might actually have *plenty of time* to prepare food and eat it reflect the great trifecta of American paucities: time, money, and spirit. Ever-increasing work hours must compensate for the decline in real earning power of flat or declining real hourly wages. A harried worker, after all, is a *dispirited* one *who will never*

---

[224]   Lim, Allen, "The Demise of the Family Meal," *The Feed Zone* (retrieved June 9, 2019) https://feedzonecookbook.com/2016/02/19/the-demise-of-the-family-meal/

ask for a raise or for improved benefits. Those who are not working and might have some available time often find themselves quite poor and possibly dependent on some social service that they might fear losing if they do not behave.

Fortunately, American Exceptionalism means that being poor establishes you as a loser, and if you are a loser, it is, of course, entirely your own fault. This remains true even if you were born into poverty, or suffered from some accident or other factor beyond your control. This is so ingrained in the American psyche that even many American poor willingly accept that poverty is *entirely their own fault.* Yes, thanks, I *will* supersize that.

18. SEX AND DRUGS AND ROCK AND ROLL, ONLY WITHOUT THE DRUGS AND ROCK AND ROLL

AMERICANS ARE SIMULTANEOUSLY SEXUALLY prudish while often adopting prurience. Thus, in the area of pornography, despite a multi-billion dollar pornographic industry and evidence that nearly 30% of Americans at work have logged into pornographic sites, only 25% of men (and 8% of women) will actually *admit* that they approve of pornography. Similarly, although around 95% of Americans have engaged in premarital sex, only 70% of men and 66% of women say that they approve of premarital sex. [225] Internally inconsistent attitudes are only the beginning of the self-defeating cycle of American sex. Sex in America, like everything else, is yet another means of social control by the oligarchs. One of the most destructive demonstrations of this is American sex education. It should come as absolutely no surprise that in those regions of the US where abstinence-only education is taught in lieu of *actual* sex education, *e.g.*, rational use of condoms and other birth control methods, teen pregnancy rates and births are substantially higher. [226] There appears to be a significant correlation between this abstinence-only education and unwanted pregnancies. Similarly irrational is how severely the US treats such idiocies as "sexting" by teenage boys (or overage adolescents like ex-

---

225   Allen, Samantha, "America's Sexual Hypocrisy Addiction," *The Daily Beast* (Apr. 14, 2017) https://www.thedailybeast.com/americas-sexual-hypocrisy-addiction
226   Stranger-Hall, Kathrin F. and Hall, David W., "Abstinence-Only Education and Teen Pregnancy Rates: Why We Need Comprehensive Sex Education in the U.S." *Public Library of Science* (Oct. 14, 2011) https://www.ncbi.nlm.nih.gov/pmc/articles/PMC3194801/

151

Congressman Anthony Weiner), compared to how it handles actual *rape*. In the US, it is notoriously difficult to obtain convictions *for rape*. Even when prosecutors obtain such convictions, it is still difficult to obtain appropriately punitive sentences for rape and sexual assault. [227]

We have already observed that the United States ranks as one of the ten most dangerous countries on Earth for women. [228] To create these rankings, the expert surveyors scored nations in six key areas: health care, sexual violence, nonsexual violence, cultural practices, discrimination, and human trafficking. The US was ranked third, tied with war-torn Syria, in terms of the danger of sexual violence, including rape, sexual harassment, coercion into sex, and the lack of access to justice in rape cases. Next worst was the war-torn Democratic Republic of Congo. For nonsexual violence—including conflict-related violence and forms of domestic physical and mental abuse—the US ranked sixth. While the US did not make the top ten in the other categories—health care, cultural practices, discrimination, and human trafficking—its high rankings in sexual and non-sexual violence against women vaulted it into the top ten, the only First World country so ranked. That sex seems so closely aligned with violence does not seem so surprising given the power dynamics of the United States. As Oscar Wilde is reputed to have said, "Everything in the world is about sex except sex. Sex is about power."

You probably get the idea. What a country.

---

227   At least one national study suggests that only 37% of reported rapes are prosecuted and only 18% of prosecuted rapes result in convictions. "What Percentage of Rape Cases Get Prosecuted? What Are The Rates of Conviction?" *Univ. of Kentucky Center for Research on Violence Against Women* (Dec. 2011) https://opsvaw.as.uky.edu/sites/default/files/07_Rape_Prosecution.pdf

228   Brennan, David, "U.S. in Top 10 Most Dangerous Countries for Women, Report Finds," *Newsweek* (June 26, 2018) https://www.newsweek.com/us-top-10-most-dangerous-countries-women-report-995229

19. Debt By a Thousand Cuts

I NDENTURED SERVITUDE BY VIRTUE of a debt owed in the US is as old as the white man's presence in North America. Originally, an indentured servant could work off their debt for the costs of transportation to North America over a period of years. In the case of indentured black people, this quickly morphed into a debt that they could never repay, *i.e.*, chattel slavery including slave status for children of the chattels.

Debtors' prisons were common in 18th- and 19th-century Britain. Debtors' prisons also existed in the early history of the US. As an aspirational matter, Article I, Section 8 (clause 4) of the United States Constitution provides that Congress shall have the power "to establish... uniform laws on the subject of bankruptcies throughout the United States." Congress did not, however, pass an act permitting voluntary bankruptcy until 1841 [Act of Aug. 19, 1841, section 1, 5 Stat. 440]. Many states and the federal government largely phased out debtors' prisons between the 1820s and the 1840s. [229]

From our discussion of American mass incarceration practices, we know that poor persons can easily find themselves in the modern equivalent of debtors' prisons for comparatively small amounts arising from the inability to raise pre-trial bail, from unpaid fines, or other fees associated with disposition of criminal cases. Debt itself can prove crushing even if it does not result in literal imprisonment.

---

[229]   Hager, Eli, "Debtors' Prisons Then and Now: FAQ," *The Marshall Project* (Feb. 24, 2015) https://www.themarshallproject.org/2015/02/24/debtors-prisons-then-and-now-faq

In the US, two major categories of debt (student debt and medical debt) are all but unknown in other parts of the world: here, American Exceptionalism is at its dystopian best!

Student debt, thanks to an act of Congress (Title 11 United States Code, Section 523), cannot be discharged in bankruptcy in the US in most cases. Student loan debt totals nearly $1.5 *trillion*, involving over 44 million borrowers. Recent American college graduates *average over $37,000 in debt* coming out of school. [230] This situation arises because of the uniquely rapacious American system of mostly non-public funding of higher education, placing most of the tuition and expense burden on students and their families. Often, the same universities that charge crushingly high tuitions are themselves immense recipients of private and government largesse for research grants and other projects.

Largely because of the availability of government-subsidized and guaranteed student loans, American colleges and universities have been raising their tuition, room, and board and other charges far above the ordinary inflation rate. For example, between 1985 and 2010, one estimate puts consumer inflation at about 115%, but *college cost inflation* is estimated at 500% over this same period. [231] Furthermore, many people who manage to graduate from a college or university with a bachelors or a graduate degree, often are faced with difficulty finding work in the field in which they studied or trained. Inability to find quality work puts further pressure on the graduate, as they try to re-pay debt that can only be disposed of by in-full payment or of course, *death*. There are also for-profit colleges and trade schools that often misrepresent the value of the training or education they provide; "Trump University" comes to mind. Nonetheless, debt incurred for even this education usually remains due, owing, and non-dischargeable in bankruptcy. Medical debt is also largely unique to the US. In the rest of the civilized

---

230   Friedman, Zack, "Can Student Loans Now Be Discharged In Bankruptcy?" *Forbes* (June 18, 2018) https://www.forbes.com/sites/zackfriedman/2018/06/18/bankruptcy-student-loans/
231   Odland, Steve, "College Costs Out of Control," *Forbes* (Mar. 24, 2012) https://www.forbes.com/sites/steveodland/2012/03/24/college-costs-are-soaring/#1abdcde11f86

world, medical debt is virtually non-existent because of *socialized medicine.* As of 2012, over *75 million* Americans were reporting problems in paying their medical bills, and over 48 million were in medical bill debt. Medical costs in the US, meanwhile, have risen 33% between 2008 and 2018, far faster than median incomes have. [232] Other major categories of household debt do exist in the rest of the civilized world, although, of course, the sheer size of the US and the magnitude of the debts make them stand out as exceptional, nonetheless. These categories include $944 billion in credit card debt, $9.27 trillion in mortgage debt, and $1.14 trillion in automobile debt. [233] This represents more than $13 trillion in household debt; the US GDP is around $20 trillion.

In the US, *everything,* including decisions to take on debt, takes place against a backdrop of the American economy's historically superior growth rates. [234] As far as most Americans workers are concerned, however, growth is over. Wages have been flat for decades, in real terms. [235] Household debt growth just to maintain a steady lifestyle has served to paper over declining returns on wages. Just as unique American issues starting with the fundamental nature of the basic American labor/management arrangement, *i.e.,* ostensible *slavery* can no longer be papered over by real growth, debt becomes particularly pernicious.

Indeed, as debt grows but income does not, we see yet another crushing and *dystopian* element added to the life of the average American.

What a country.

---

232   Biehle, Sean, "2019 Medical Billing Statistics," *MedData* (Feb. 5, 2019) https://www.meddata.com/blog/2017/10/26/medical-billing-statistics/
233   Tsosie, Claire and El Issa, Erin, "2018 American Household Credit Card Debt Study," *NerdWallet* (Dec. 10, 2018) https://www.nerdwallet.com/blog/average-credit-card-debt-household/
234   Indeed, it is my supposition of this work that spectacular economic growth permitted the papering over of most of the exceptionally draconian working arrangements and lack of benefits provided in the American work place.
235   DeSilver, Drew, "For most U.S. workers, real wages have barely budged for decades," *Pew Research Center* (Aug. 7, 2018) https://www.pewresearch.org/fact-tank/2018/08/07/for-most-us-workers-real-wages-have-barely-budged-for-decades/

20. Courthouse Jesters

SOMEONE CAN WALK OR drive around virtually any major city in the world outside of the US and ponder the fact that the local people seem to have more relaxed expressions on their faces than Americans do. Unlike Americans, such people probably do not have to worry that a simple accident might result in both injury and in their financial ruination. One's own crippling medical costs are bad enough in the American system, but thanks to the ever-arbitrary American legal system, one might have to pay the medical costs of the alleged victim, plus litigation costs. In many ways, at least for the relatively powerless, the US is a litigation trap, although just how bad this is varies from state to state, or even county to county. According to one estimate, the US spends around 2% of its *entire GDP* on litigation costs, with about half of that going to attorneys and their costs. [236] Another study suggests that four out of five of the world's lawyers reside in the US. [237] A Harvard study suggests that the exceptionally litigious reputation of Americans and their courts does not result from the handling of routine disputes, but rather is caused by spectacular results in the areas of class actions and punitive damages. [238] Any individual or business, or non-profit,

---

236   Rubin, Paul H., "More Money Into Bad Suits," *The New York Times* (Nov. 16, 2010) https://www.nytimes.com/roomfordebate/2010/11/15/investing-in-someone-elses-lawsuit/more-money-into-bad-suits
237   Danzig, Christopher, "Infographic of the Day: American Litigiousness Statistics That Will Make You Angry," *Above the Law* (July 17, 2012) https://abovethelaw.com/2012/07/infographic-of-the-day-american-litigiousness-statistics-that-will-make-you-angry/
238   Ramseyer, Mark J. and Rasmusen. Eric B., "Comparative Litigation Rates," *Harvard/John M. Olin Center for Law, Economics and Business* (Nov. 2010) http://www.law.harvard.edu/programs/olin_center/papers/pdf/Ramseyer_681.pdf

for that matter, may, assuming they have deep enough pockets to be targeted for litigation in the first place, be tagged for such a potentially spectacular result against it *at any time for any reason.* For good measure, the defensive litigant must incur its own legal fees at its own expense, legal fees which may ultimately be every bit as crippling as an ultimate loss in the litigation.

Much of this particular area of American Exceptionalism can be attributed to the American "rugged individualist" mentality. A typical American might view "rolling the dice" for the possibility of a big verdict as more desirable than settlement. In the rest of the world, refusing to settle could result in a serious loss of face by selfishly subjecting others to your dirty laundry. Also unique to the US is that a huge component of damages in personal injury cases is the medical expense that must be borne by individuals, an expense that is invariably socialized in the rest of the world.

In fields such as medicine, accounting, or even the law itself, extraordinary measures are taken to practice professions "defensively," lest one suffer a massive and enterprise-destroying or career-ending malpractice award. In medicine, the costs of defensive practices to stave off litigation as opposed to direct costs of defending actual litigation are estimated to be in the tens of billions of dollars [239] or even in the hundreds of billions of dollars per year. [240] Despite the high costs of litigation avoidance in medicine, the number of Americans dying as a result of medical mistake is still remarkably high, estimated to number as many as hundreds of thousands per year. (*see* footnote 65). Because moneyed interests have captured the American political establishment, resort to litigation to solve social problems in the American context is also legendary. Interestingly, occasional experiments in the use of actual "problem-solving courts" such as juvenile or family courts, drug courts and the like, designed

---

239   Rothberg, Michael M., et als., "The Cost of Defensive Medicine on Three Hospital Medicine Services," *Journal of the American Medical Association Internal Medicine* (Nov. 1, 2014) https://jamanetwork.com/journals/jamainternalmedicine/fullarticle/1904758
240   "Physician Study: Quantifying the Cost of Defensive Medicine, Lawsuit-Driven Medicine Creates $650-$850 Billion Annual Health Care Costs," *Jackson Health Care* (retrieved June 12, 2019) https://jacksonhealth care.com/media-room/surveys/defensive-medicine-study-2010/

to address specific community issues have shown inconclusive or dubious results. [241] On a larger scale, the "problem solving" of courts with respect to broader systemic social issues such as environmental matters, for example, has proven even more problematic. To be sure, many other liberal democratic countries address the bulk of their social problems through their *legislative* processes, rather than their courts, but then, America. As we have discussed, the US as a whole is an oligarchy that is almost entirely unresponsive to the will of the public where that will is inconsistent with the interests of the moneyed and powerful (*see* footnote 1). In addition, most Americans have a fundamental misunderstanding of what their courts are actually supposed to do. Lost in the "teaser" of the large, lottery-like "runaway verdicts" is the irony of a system that, in its adjudication of both civil and criminal cases, overwhelmingly serves to *preserve the status quo* and, ultimately, to protect the interests of the moneyed and the powerful. [242] It is no accident that the key doctrine of American courts is *stare decisis*, a Latin term signifying that courts must follow the earlier decisions of higher courts before them. This supposedly provides consistency and relative certainty based on court decisions of the past.

Then again, it might surprise people to learn that judicial review, the most vaunted power of the United States courts to strike down laws passed by Congress and signed by the President, is found nowhere in the Constitution itself. Indeed, the Supreme Court did not even exercise this supposed power of judicial review for the first fifteen years of its existence.

Then, in the famous case of *Marbury v. Madison*, 5 U.S. 137 (1803), the Supreme Court pronounced that indeed, the courts,

---

241   Appell, Annette Ruth, "Introduction: The Promise and Pitfalls of Social Problem Solving Through the Courts and Legal Advocacy," 31 Wash.U. J. L. & Pol'y 001 (2009) https://openscholarship. wustl.edu/law_journal_law_policy/vol31/iss1/2/
242   Part of the wild-card nature of civil litigation is the jury system itself (especially in civil cases). The civil jury system ensures that the most uninformed members of the public dispense what are potentially the most arbitrary outcomes possible to those who put their faith in the legal system. If powerful-enough interests (corporate America, for example) *actually* find themselves threatened, however, one would expect trial judges or appeals courts to *correct* "excessive verdicts" from "runaway juries."

especially the Supreme Court, do have this power after all. The specific context of *Marbury* arose from the appointment of so-called "midnight judges" by John Adams just as he was leaving the presidency, but the specifics matter less than the principle itself, *i.e.*, unelected judges can invalidate laws duly enacted by an elected Congress and President based solely on their own opinion as to "constitutional intent."

Having thus established the principle of judicial review in *Marbury*, curiously, the Supreme Court did not exercise it again for decades, using it for the second time in the infamous case of *Dred Scott v. Sandford*, 60 U.S. (19 How.) 393 (1857). There, the Supreme Court invalidated laws permitting a slave brought into free territory from obtaining his freedom. The Civil War ensued shortly thereafter.

After *Dred Scott*, the lower federal courts and Supreme Court were much less reticent about exercising this power of judicial review.

To be sure, the occasional landmark civil rights cases such as *Brown v. Bd. of Education of Topeka*, 347 U.S. 483 (1954) do create the impression that American courts are engaging in the granting of rights drawn from the benevolent Constitution for the betterment of all. I cannot emphasize how helpful this sort of thing is to the overall mission of keeping the peasants in line.

Nonetheless, the broader reality of High Court *jurisprudence* is more mundane (and more "on mission"). Long before the case of *Citizens United v. Federal Election Commission*, 558 U.S. 310 (2010) opened the floodgates for corporate money to spill into the electoral process, the Court was long engaged in advancing the status of the American business corporation in all respects, particularly in the area of corporate "personhood." [243] Indeed, long before Mitt Romney famously told us that "corporations are people, my friend" and long before Charlton Heston told us that *soylent green is people*, the Supreme Court used the Fourteenth Amendment of

---

243   Torres-Spelliscy, Ciara, "The History of Corporate Personhood," *Brennan Center for Justice* (Apr. 7, 2014) https://www.brennancenter.org/blog/hobby-lobby-argument

the Constitution to treat corporations as people. [244] You may recall that the Fourteenth Amendment was a post-Civil War Amendment intended to grant equal protection of law to black people. Nonetheless, over the years, Republican courts managed to find a way *not* to extend equal protection of law to black people. These same courts did manage, however, to use the Fourteenth Amendment to protect the moneyed agglomerations known as corporations by, of course, treating them as "people."

The institutions of American law often function in this subtle way. The rich and powerful ultimately prevail, but, because the legal dispensations reach the public through aging people wearing aging black robes holding court in aging replicas of Greek and Roman temples, the public, at least, believes that these decisions are based on fairness and justice.

What a country.

---

244   Pruitt, Sarah, "How the 14th Amendment Made Corporations into 'People'," *History. com* (Oct. 15, 2018) https://www.history.com/news/14th-amendment-corporate-personhood-made-corporations-into-people

21. WASTE NOT...
WHY DO YOU HATE AMERICA?

T
HE UNITED STATES PRODUCES around 40% of the world's waste despite representing only around 5% of the world's population. [245] Along the way, Americans also consume somewhere between 17% [246] and 20% of the world's energy. [247]

We start our discussion with motor fuels. The United States has more private automobiles and light trucks for personal use than it does licensed drivers. [248] We have already discussed "life" in the American suburbs, which often features a paucity of public transportation or even sidewalks resulting in the most basic of transactions, children going to school, acquiring groceries and household items, commuting to work, visiting loved ones and friends, invariably requiring a privately owned motor vehicle. Hence, in the United States, people walk less, interact with other people less, and are required to devote a significant portion of their income to the acquisition, insurance and maintenance costs of their vehicles plus fuel and tolls where applicable. The consequence of the American suburban set-up requires ever-increasing energy consumption for

---

245   Dean, Signe, "Watch: Here's How the American Lifestyle Really Compares to The Rest of The World," *Science Alert* (Sep. 8, 2017) https://www.sciencealert.com/here-s-how-the-american-lifestyle-really-compares-to-the-rest-of-the-world

246   "How much of the world's energy does the United States use?" *American Geosciences Institute* (retrieved June 12, 2019) https://www.americangeosciences.org/critical-issues/faq/how-much-worlds-energy-does-united-states-use

247   "Population and Energy Consumption," *World Population Balance* (retrieved June 12, 2019) https://www.worldpopulationbalance.org/population_energy

248   "More Cars than Drivers in U.S.," *Road and Track* (Nov. 6, 2012) https://www.roadandtrack.com/car-culture/a9672/more-cars-than-drivers-in-us/

transportation and housing. Detached homes have more surfaces to radiate energy, and the recent trend to "McMansions" leads to even greater home heating and cooling needs in this sector.

Vast amounts of energy are required to build and maintain a network of utility lines and the armada of vehicles necessary to maintain them, as well as a plethora of power stations, gasoline fueling stations, and so forth. As we move from the energy needed to run homes and vehicles, to the energy people need to function (that would be food), we see the same trend toward profligate use. Indeed, Americans *throw out approximately half of the food produced in the country.* [249] Many Americans have a vague understanding, helped along by package "sell-by" dates, that their throwing out food has something to do with food safety. In fact, like many other things in the American market place, food disposal practices are mostly about aesthetics and marketing. [250]

Just as "you are what you eat," Madison Avenue tells us that "clothes make the man." Sorry to be gender-specific; I did not invent that slogan! Thus, it should come as no surprise that Americans are excellent at wasting textiles and clothing items. The amount of such textiles disposed of—80 lbs or over 35 kg—*by every American every year* represents approximately half the body weight of an average sized person, a world "best." [251]

Aggregated together, Americans generate over 250 million tons of overall trash *per year* or a staggering 1,400 lbs. (over 600 kg) *per person per year.* [252] Heaven forbid that this is the end of it, *i.e.,* the garbage will eventually rot in a landfill and form something reusable. Of course, it will not. Plastics represent almost 13% of this total of

249   Chandler, Adam, "Why Americans Lead the World in Food Waste," *The Atlantic* (July 15, 2016) https://www.theatlantic.com/business/archive/2016/07/american-food-waste/491513/
250   Ohio State University, "Why Americans waste so much food: Most people feel guilty about discarding food, but say it would be hard to stop," *Science Daily* (July 21, 2016) https://www.sciencedaily.com/releases/2016/07/160721151231.htm
251   Cline, Elizabeth, "Op-Ed: America Leads the World in Textile Waste and Unwanted Clothing: Here's Why," *Pratt/ Brooklyn Fashion and Design Accelerator* (July 26, 2016) https://bkaccelerator.com/america-leads-world-textile-waste-unwanted-clothing/
252   Breyer, Melissa, "Trash by the numbers: Startling statistics about US garbage," *Treehugger. com* (July 1, 2016) https://www.treehugger.com/environmental-policy/trash-numbers-startling-statistics-about-americans-and-their-garbage.html

American generated waste, or around 200 lbs. (90 kg) per person per year. [253] Tragically much of this ends up in the oceans and even inside of fish and in whales' bellies.

In order to generate all the goodies that Americans waste, we start with a lot of land used to grow food. According to the United States Department of Agriculture, there are nearly 2.2 billion acres of American land area. [254] Of this, cropland (mostly grains) consumes 391,975,000 acres; grassland pasture and range (mostly cattle, sheep, and other critters) consumes 655,486,000 acres; forest-use land consumes 631,682,000 acres; special-use land (whatever that is) consumes 315,872,000 acres; urban areas consume 69,864,000 acres; and miscellaneous other land uses consume 195,542,000 acres. Total agricultural uses—cropland, grassland/pasture, and forests—represent around 1.7 billion of the 2.2 billion acres, or most of the land area of the United States. American agricultural processes are themselves incredibly energy and resource-intensive. One of the key resources used in these processes is water, which Americans also waste prodigiously. [255]

All of this "production" followed by all of this waste creates a mindset in Americans that they are *so prosperous* that they can afford to *throw away more each year* than most people on Earth have ever had or, indeed, will ever have. In fact, the purpose of this dispensation is to compensate Americans for their being among the poorest people in the world *when measured in what actually matters:* time to themselves, actual freedom, the ability to interact with loved ones and friends, and agency over their own productive lives, or indeed, over their lives themselves. Thus, Americans are the only industrialized country that *does not require that its workers*

---

253   "Municipal Solid Waste", U.S. Environmental Protection Agency (archive) (last updated March 29, 2016) https://archive.epa.gov/epawaste/nonhaz/municipal/web/html/
254   "Major Land Uses", U.S. Dept. of Agriculture Economic Research Service (retrieved June 6, 2019) https://www.ers.usda.gov/data-products/major-land-uses.aspx
255   "Water and agriculture: Managing water sustainably is key to the future of food and agriculture," *OECD.org* (accessed June 6, 2019) http://www.oecd.org/agriculture/topics/water-and-agriculture/

have paid vacations. [256] As a result, Americans receive among the least mandatory paid time off, vacation or otherwise, in the world, if not the least. [257]

The compensation is *the stuff.* Hence, Americans have really big houses if they aren't homeless, large, gas-guzzling cars if they can still afford gas and insurance, or a car, and *more food* than anyone else on Earth, over 3,600 calories per day, making the United States number one in food-calorie consumption, along with being a world leader in obesity. [258] As of the early 21st century, the pernicious effects of Americans' voracious appetite for material goods amidst the actual misery of their overworked and underappreciated lives are having real and likely irreversible consequences for Americans themselves, for the other 95% of humanity, and for every living organism on Earth.

The litany of these horrors includes industrial pollution from which we "enjoy" cancers, asthma, and heart/respiratory problems, among many others, and the *big kahuna* of problems, climate change, which threatens weather and climate stability, and sea level rise which threatens urban areas, arable land, and regular growing seasons. In turn, the world "enjoys" political instability as people must move just to survive as their own regions become unlivable. For good measure, the Earth suffers a massive species die off and attendant loss of biodiversity.

We come full circle.

As I write this in 2019, it appears that the system of bribing Americans for stealing their lives by plying them with *stuff,* much of it cheap and disposable garbage manufactured abroad, especially in

---

256   Mohn, Tanya, "U.S. The Only Advanced Economy That Does Not Require Employers To Provide Paid Vacation Time, Report Says," *Forbes* (Aug. 13, 2013) https://www.forbes.com/sites/tanyamohn/2013/08/13/paid-time-off-forget-about-it-a-report-looks-at-how-the-u-s-compares-to-other-countries/#39fd4c1f6f65

257   Gadd, Michael, "Americans get the least paid vacation time in the world – while other countries enjoy as many as FORTY days off a year," *Daily Mail* (Aug. 21, 2014) https://www.dailymail.co.uk/news/article-2730947/Americans-paid-vacation-time-world-countries-enjoy-FORTY-days-year.html

258   Staff Reporter, "Calorie Counting: Countries Who Consume Most Per Person," *HNGN* (Oct. 23, 2014) http://www.hngn.com/articles/46900/20141023/calorie-counting-countries-who-consume-most-per-person.htm

China, is actually going to *destroy everything, forever*. Nonetheless, American Exceptionalism does not permit *any* level of introspection, let alone questioning of the basic premises of the system *even to save the system itself*.

Some Americans of goodwill are clear-minded enough to recognize that the world is full of horrors, but it is nonetheless our duty to save what we can of the world's beauty. For its part, American Exceptionalism envisions a world where it is more imperative to waste every ounce of the lifeblood of all but the richest and most powerful, in the name of profit, of course. Thus, the highest value is to squander resources *as fast as possible*, in an endless cycle of frenetic effort by the peasants and slaves who will not have the time or energy for the *actual* betterment of their own lives. Even *dreaming* of taking on the oligarchs who oppress the peasants is unthinkable. A system this ugly can only produce ugliness itself. This is what American Exceptionalism has *really wrought*. The ugliness of wasted beauty, the ugliness of garbage, the ugliness of unhappy and unfulfilled anxiety-ridden lives, the ugliness of uninspired landscapes of strip malls and fast-food outlets and gasoline stations and paved-over everything. American Exceptionalism has placed the ugliness of a fast-food meal scarfed down in a moving vehicle passing an endless series of strip malls at the *omega point of human achievement*.

We arrive at a one-off crisis point that the human race has never before encountered. Because the American empire is the first truly global empire, its exhaustion point includes the very real possibility of exhausting *everything*, and taking the rest of the planet with it. Thanks to a remarkably effective combination of Hollywood propaganda and capitalist attitude adjustment of the rest of the world, there currently are no operating counter-models of industrial capitalist living on an environmentally sustainable basis. Western Europe is merely less bad than the US. The so-called Third World is, in the best American tradition, aspiring to use more resources to advance its own consumer-based economies.

As more and more scientists and United Nations' officials tell us we are running out of time to ameliorate the worst impacts of climate change, the harsh reality is that we are largely out of time already. In the American Exceptionalism mythos, more is always better, even if it makes people miserable. Indeed, even the supposed beneficiaries, *the rich*, are less happy *themselves* when income and wealth disparity hit ever-widening levels. [259]

Nonetheless, American Exceptionalism dictates that the American system is the greatest system ever created, and we simply cannot question it *in any aspect*. Thus, it does not appear that we will be able to change *this mindset*. We will certainly not change it in time to alter the behaviors and structures necessary to ameliorate the worst impacts resulting from decades and centuries of *prior* American Exceptionalism and industrial capitalism, in general. Physicist Max Planck suggested that science advances "one funeral at a time." Unfortunately, we have a generation of privileged older Americans inured to American Exceptionalism who have no sense of obligation to the future; one funeral at a time will not be fast enough, I am afraid. Even the less-privileged American peasants *think* they are in an advantaged position in the "greatest country in the world" and refuse to relinquish even their own pathetic "privileges" and their "stuff," even as they are drowning in it.

Like it or not, anything that cannot go on indefinitely will not go on indefinitely. We will come to a crash point. There is strong evidence that we have already come to a number of crash points. Politically, populist leaders (others would call them by the more accurate term reflecting the merger of monopoly capitalism and state power, *i.e.*, fascists) have been elected in the United States, the Philippines, Brazil, and Hungary. White nationalist parties are gaining ground in large parts of Europe and apparently in the US. On the environmental side, much of the world, including the United

---

259   Ingraham, Christopher, "How rising inequality hurts everyone, even the rich," *Washington Post* (Feb. 6, 2018) https://www.washingtonpost.com/news/wonk/wp/2018/02/06/how-rising-inequality-hurts-everyone-even-the-rich/?utm_term=.5e2a75c38498

States itself, has been "enjoying" extreme weather events, including stronger hurricanes, wildfires, droughts, floods, heat waves, and cold snaps. Water tables are depleting just as rainfall is getting less reliable. Populations appear to be cresting just as antibiotic-resistant germs are taking hold. At the very same moment, certain communities have suddenly succumbed to the belief that vaccinating their children against preventable diseases is an unacceptable intrusion on their "freedom." In a classic display of American Exceptionalism, the United States has even pulled out of the Paris Climate Accords. [260] This is exactly the kind of self-defeating, arrogant gesture that we could expect only from American Exceptionalism.

Here we are. You are welcome to despair. I strongly suggest, however, that you think in terms of the one thing you can control. That, of course, is *your own course of action* and, for good measure, your own response to events. It might also include the actions of your own loved ones, if you are very persuasive. This is the moment to realize that the existential angst you have been feeling all this time really *is not about you or your own inadequacies.* You are simply a member of a society, and a social, economic, and political system whose very purpose is to degrade and destroy you, and all for the benefit of a tiny group of rich and powerful people who have no more regard for you than they would for an earthworm or a moth. Does that make you feel better?

Back to our story. Perhaps you believe that some of the worst brunt of what American Exceptionalism has wrought will be in the hollowed-out confines of the United States itself, and you want to get out while you still can. While places like Bangladesh and sub-Saharan Africa and a number of Pacific islands will likely fare worse than many parts of North America, a social order based on the mean-spirited rugged individualism of Ayn Rand is bad enough for most people, even in times of abundance and growth. It will

260   Shear, Michael D., "Trump Will Withdraw U.S. from Paris Climate Agreement," *The New York Times* (June 1, 2017) https://www.nytimes.com/2017/06/01/climate/trump-paris-climate-agreement.html

prove disastrous and without doubt, *lethal* in times of decline, just as it did during the Great Depression. While I cannot suggest a particular destination, I can suggest that you will probably fare better somewhere that is not in the permanent throes of American Exceptionalism and all that goes with it, and that will probably be somewhere that is not the United States of America.

I would strongly encourage this. The fewer people who remain to fight for the dwindling resources in what is left of the United States, the better. You may wish to go off the grid to some individually sustainable lifestyle within the borders of the US. I would admire you for this effort; perhaps you can even band together in some kind of sustainable community. Such models of survivability would be extremely helpful. Be warned that this might be a very uncomfortable situation. Because the success of such a project would mean you were not still their slaves, the surviving forces of American capitalism will align to thwart any and all such projects, particularly if they achieve any kind of scale.

Finally, with your improved knowledge of just how "exceptional" the American system really is, some among you may wish to try to reform it. I wish you the best of luck. You would be venturing into an area where many have tried and few have succeeded over a period of centuries. You would be doing so at a time when powerful moneyed interests have captured virtually all of the instruments and levers of power within the American system. These people would sooner initiate nuclear war than pay an inheritance tax.

Perhaps revolution is possible. I remain agnostic as to whether revolution actually *is* possible in the American context, and I am agnostic as to what form "the revolution" must take. Fundamental changes to the political, economic and social antecedents of the American system just seem unlikely to me. I am not alone in thinking this. [261]

I anticipate that the United States will continue its lengthy slide

---

261   In a quote attributed to Mark Fisher, "It is easier to imagine an end to the world than an end to capitalism." *see* Fisher, Mark, "Capitalist realism: is there no alternative?" Zero Books (2009).

into penury and irrelevance for some time. Indeed, this process may take decades more to fully play out. I am certain that, as the decline unfolds, the propaganda of American Exceptionalism will step up, and the powerful will deploy every conceivable, available technology, from social media and smart phones to old school billboards and sound trucks to disseminate the message. The message, of course, is that the United States of America is the greatest country in the history of the universe as God Himself has so decreed.

You know that believing the message is simply not in your personal interest, or in anyone's personal interest. Unless, of course, you are an oligarch. People of the United States unite! You have nothing to lose but your place on the food chain as some oligarch's lunch.

Better yet, just get the hell out while you still can.

ABOUT THE AUTHOR

Shortly before the inauguration of Donald J. Trump as the 45th President of the United States in January of 2017, my daughter ("Ivanka J. Putin") and our then house guest (we will call him "A") thought that it would be amusing if I took to ranting on Twitter. This is the very same platform that Mr. Trump himself regularly uses for his own highly successful political rants.

Thus, with their help, particularly the technical prowess of young Ivanka, Donald J. Putin (http://twitter.com/donald_j_putin) came into being just days before our 45th "president" was sworn in. Ivanka is also responsible for the cool *book cover*.

Some tens of thousands of individual Twitter rants later, and with over ten-thousand Twitter followers, Donald J. Putin regularly rails rhapsodic on the issues of the day.

Donald J. Putin lives in Brooklyn, NY, with his wife Mrs. Putin, daughter Ivanka J. and a couple of cats. His interests include vodka, global domination, and chronicling the end-stages of American empire.